The
Puerto Ricans

ETHNIC CHRONOLOGY SERIES
NUMBER 11

The
Puerto Ricans
1493-1973
A Chronology & Fact Book

Compiled and edited by

Francesco Cordasco

With

Eugene Bucchioni

1973
OCEANA PUBLICATIONS, INC.
DOBBS FERRY, NEW YORK

Library of Congress Catalog Card Number 73-5840

ISBN 0-379-00509-3

Manufactured in the United States of America

In Memory Of

Luis Muñoz Rivera (1859 - 1916)

TABLE OF CONTENTS

EDITOR'S FOREWORD

There is little doubt that Puerto Ricans should be included in an "Ethnic Series," addressed to American readers; yet this could be hazardous if Puerto Rican history and the Puerto Rican experience on the mainland are defined in those terms which see the Puerto Rican identity as essentially that of other ethnic groups: the peril lies in failing to note at the outset that the Puerto Rican/United States experience is unlike that of any other group, and that even the appellation "Puerto Rican Americans" carries with it an incongrousness which damages historical reality. The Jesuit sociologist, Rev. Joseph P. Fitzpatrick, struggled with this problem, and has best placed it into focus:

> The Puerto Ricans have come for the most part in the first great airborne migration of people from abroad; they are decidedly newcomers of the aviation age. A Puerto Rican can travel from San Juan to New York in less time than a New Yorker could travel from Coney Island to Times Square a century ago. They are the first group to come in large numbers from a different cultural background, but who are, nevertheless, citizens of the United States. They are the first group of newcomers who bring a cultural practice of widespread intermingling and intermarriage of peoples of many different colors. They are the first group of predominantly Catholic migrants not accompanied by a native clergy. Numerous characteristics of the Puerto Ricans make their migration unique."[1]

It is the uniqueness of the Puerto Rican experience which presents both an opportunity and a challenge; and it might be cogently argued (as Father Fitzpatrick notes) that even before large scale migration to the United States mainland occurred, Puerto Ricans had been facing a crisis of national and cultural identity. How could it have been otherwise? For some four centuries Puerto Rico had been part of the Spanish Empire; and when, in the latter part of the 19th century, concomitant with the decline of Spanish imperial power, Puerto Rico found itself on the verge of a new and essentially independent governance, it was drawn into the expanding orbit of the United States. In the sense of the continuing search

for national and cultural identity, Puerto Ricans are truly unique in that
curious amalgam which is American society: concepts such as cultural
pluralism, or assimilation, as applied to other ethnic groups, do not as
easily apply to Puerto Ricans.[2]

A large literature on the Puerto Rican United States mainland experience exists;[3] and this literature is an attestation of the Puerto Rican
presence in American society, of the influence of the evolving identity of
the Puerto Rican community on the mainland.[4] This volume provides a
dimensionally compact collection of materials which places in clear perspective the experience of Puerto Ricans on the United States mainland
and the historical backgrounds which make this experience intelligible:
more often than not the island's relationships with the United States (a
relationship still undergoing change) furnish the historical framework in
which the mainland experience is to be more completely understood.

I have included materials from the important and generally unavail-
able Report of the United States/Puerto Rico Commission on the Status
of Puerto Rico. The Commission was convened in 1964 to "study all factors. . . . which may have a bearing on the present and future relationships between the United States and Puerto Rico," and published its
Report in 1966. From the Report, I have chosen those sections which
provide historical backgrounds, which undertake to explore the legal relationships (vis-à-vis prospective change), and which detailedly enumer-
ate the conclusions and recommendations of the Commission. Luis
Muñoz Marín's "Puerto Rico Since Columbus" and Joseph Monserrat's
"Puerto Rico's Contributions to America's Prosperity" furnish (deriving
as they do, from the 1950s and early 1960s) insightful views of a rapidly
changing Puerto Rico following the assumption of Commonwealth status
in 1952; and the history of the migration to the United States mainland
and its changing patterns are delineated in the materials drawn from the
invaluable unpublished report/construct prepared by the Puerto Rican
Forum of New York City; and in the important presentation of Joseph
Monserrat (at the time, Director of the Migration Division, Commonwealth of Puerto Rico) at Howard University in 1968.

The Puerto Rican experience on the mainland is lucidly articulated
in the material/report on Puerto Ricans in New York City: essentially,
the urban experience elsewhere in the United States would not be significantly different. The New York City Puerto Rican community numbers
over 800,000 persons according to the 1970 Federal census, a figure itself contested by the Migration Division of the Commonwealth of Puerto
Rico which has set the figure for New York City at 1.2 million Puerto
Ricans.[5] For the Puerto Rican experience in mainland schools (the most
sensitive of all social institutions for a new people), I have included my

introductory essay to the recently reissued Puerto Rican Study: A Report
on the Education and Adjustment of Puerto Rican Pupils in the Public
Schools of the City of New York. The Puerto Rican Study is one of the
most comprehensive statements yet made, not only of the Puerto Rican
school experience, but of the educational experience of the non-English
speaking minority child in the American school. The chronology (to the
best of my knowledge, the most complete available in English) is as
comprehensive as I could make it, but inevitably some important events
will have been missed.

I am indebted to the many individuals whose counsel I have sought in
preparing the volume; intended as it is for a wide range of American
students who are studying Puerto Rican relationships with the United
States, it will hopefully serve as a basic resource text in courses in
Puerto Rican studies, ethnic relations, minority groups in the United
States, urban sociology, and current American history. Equally, it
makes available to libraries a collection of basic materials; and it
should be of value, in the expanding awareness of Puerto Rico and the
Puerto Rican community on the mainland, to a wide sonstituency outside
traditional academic contexts. My colleague, Dr. Eugene Bucchioni,
with whom I have worked in urban barrios, supplied invaluable aid in the
volume's compilation; and Pablo Rivera Alvarez (who has lived both the
island and mainland experience) checked all of the materials in his role
as discerning critic and friend. Angela B. Jack assumed the onerous
tasks of typing and date verification for the chronology.

Francesco Cordasco
Montclair State College

Former Consultant,
Migration Division,
Commonwealth of
Puerto Rico

[1] Joseph P. Fitzpatrick, Puerto Rican Americans: The Meaning of
Migration to the Mainland (Englewood Cliffs, N. J.: Prentice-Hall, 1971),
p. 2.

[2] See, in this connection, Manuel Mandonado-Denis, Puerto Rico: A
Socio-Historic Interpretation (New York: Random House, 1972). "The
problems faced by a Puerto Rican in his society are magnified and multiplied when he migrates to the United States. Regardless of what Glazer

and Moynihan argue in Beyond the Melting Pot, the American ethic is a
messianic one, and all ethnic groups are required to assimilate culturally as a condition for achieving a share in the material and spiritual
goods of American society. This is particularly true for Puerto Ricans,
whose process of assimilation to what Glazer and Moynihan call the
"Anglo-Saxon Center" starts in the Island of Puerto Rico itself. The intellectual and moral colonization of Puerto Ricans is merely continued
and intensified on the mainland, but what I have called elsewhere 'the
colonialist syndrome' is the result of a deliberate policy on the part of
the American and the colonial government geared towards the destruction of the trend in Puerto Rican society that has historically been the
main obstacle to the complete cultural assimilation of our country:
namely, the trend towards independence." (pp. 319-320)

[3]A guide to the literature is F. Cordasco, E. Bucchioni, and D. Cas-
tellanos, Puerto Ricans on the United States Mainland: A Bibliography of
Reports, Texts, Critical Studies and Related Materials (Totowa, N. J.:
Rowman & Littlefield, 1972). "The six sections of the bibliography com-
prehend a representative register of titles which afford a fully dimen-
sional overview of bibliographical resources; of the migration to the
mainland; of the island experience ...; of the mainland experience deriving from the dynamics of conflict and acculturation; of the multitudinous
educational experiments (encapsulated often in the new attention born in
Johnsonian America to the culture of the poor and the massive programmatic onslaughts on poverty, and not unrelated to the subtle shifts from
civil rights and integration [following Black models] to an emphasis on
Puerto Rican power and community solidarity); and of that experience
from the contexts of social needs which encompass health, housing, employment, and other human needs." (p. xiii)

[4]Much of the literature is available in F. Cordasco and E. Bucchioni,
The Puerto Rican Experience: A Sociological Sourcebook (Totowa, N.J.:
Rowman & Littlefield, 1973); and in F. Cordasco and E. Bucchioni, The
Puerto Rican Community and its Children on the Mainland: A Sourcebook
for Teachers, Social Workers and other Professionals (Metuchen, N. J.:
Scarecrow Press, 1972, 2nd ed.).

[5]See the New York Times, April 20, 1972. In a final report on 1970
Hispanic population figures, the Census Bureau listed 846,731 Puerto
Ricans in New York City; the total mainland Puerto Rican population was
reported as 1,430,000. These final figures include those born in Puerto
Rico or having a parent born there, and (for the New York City figure)
third generation Puerto Ricans, i.e., children born on the mainland to
Puerto Ricans also born on the mainland. See New York Times, March
5, 1973.

CHRONOLOGY

CHRONOLOGY

1493	On November 19, Christopher Columbus discovers the island of Borikén on his second trip to the New World and calls it San Juan Bautista.
1508	Juan Ponce de León is made Governor of the island and founds the first settlement, called Caparra.
1509	The seat of government is moved and called Ciudad de Puerto Rico.
1521	The capital city is renamed San Juan, and the island takes the name of the capital: Puerto Rico.
1530	With the limited gold supply exhausted, many colonizers are attracted to Peru; others devote themselves to agriculture.
1595	Sir Francis Drake's fleet attacks San Juan but is rebuffed.
1598	George Clifford, the Count of Cumberland, captures San Juan with 4,000 men and holds it from June through November.
1625	Dutch fleet attacks San Juan on September 24, but is rebuffed after its troops sack the city.
1631	Construction begins on the massive El Morro Fortress to protect the city.
1660	Governor Pérez de Guzmán writes to the King that "eleven years have passed since the last ship came to this island."
1680	The city of Ponce is founded on the south coast.
1746-1759	Land reforms of Ferdinand VI contributed to a population increase and facilitated the settlement of the interior of the island.
1760	Mayagüez is founded on the west coast.
1765	Publication of Alexandro O'Reilly's Memoria a SM Sobre la Isla de Puerto (in Coll y Toste, Boletín Historico, VIII, 108-124). Don Alejandro O'Reylly traveled through Puerto Rico on a survey for the Spanish Crown.

1775   Population is 70,250, including 6,467 black slaves.

1778   The Crown forced to grant complete rights of private ownership in land. Before the 18th century, all land in Puerto Rico was nominally owned by the Crown.

       The Royal Cédula of January 14, provided for the division and granting of royal lands with the right of freehold.

       Publication of one of the most important primary sources on Puerto Rican 18th century history: Inigo Abbad y La Sierra, Historia Geografica, Civil y Natural de la Isla de San Juan Bautista de Puerto Rico (Madrid: Imp. de Don Antonio Espinosa, 1788); reissued with notes by Luis M. Díaz Soles: Editionces de la Universidad de Puerto Rico, 1959. Abbad y La Sierra was a Benedictine monk who lived in Puerto Rico for several years during the 1770s.

1790   Birth year of Rafael Cordero y Molina (1790-1868), Puerto Rican pioneer educator who opened a free school to teach the poor.

1797   San Juan is attacked by the British, who retire after a one month siege.

1799   The Spanish Crown approved the establishment of new towns, among them Cayey, Faryado, Caguas, Aguadilla, Rincón, Moca, and La Vega or Naranjal. See Cayetano Coll y Toste, Boletín Historico de Puerto Rico, I (1914), pp. 239-310.

1800   Population of Puerto Rico is estimated as 155,406; by 1899, it was 953,243.

1808   Under the Constitutional Monarchy of 1808, Puerto Ricans were invited to name a representative to the central governing council of the Kingdom. See Adolfo de Hostos, Ciudad Murada (Habana: Lex, 1948).

1812   Ramón Power represents the island in the Spanish Cortes.

1815   The Cédula de Gracias opens Puerto Rico to immigration from other Catholic countries than Spain and from other parts of the Empire.

1821   First of the 19th century slave rebellions took place in
                Bayamón. Slave rebellions occurred in Guayama (1822);
                in Ponce (1826); in Toa Baja (1843); in Ponce and Vega
                Baja (1848). See Salvador Brau, Historia de Puerto Rico
                (New York: Appleton, 1904).

1822-1837   Tyrannical governorship of Miguel de la Torre which
                strictly regulated the lives of citizens. De la Torre was
                the Spanish Commander defeated by Simon Bolivar in the
                battle of Carabobo, Venezuela in 1821.

1824   The Bando de Policía y Buen Gobierno authorized the
                arrest of "vagrants" and their employment on public
                works or in the military unless they were gainfully em-
                ployed otherwise. (See Salvador Brau, Historia de
                Puerto Rico, New York: Appleton, 1904).

1827   Birth year of Ramón Emeterio Betances (1827-1898), great
                abolitionist and Puerto Rican patriot.

1832   Publication of important early narrative of George D.
                Flinter, A View of the Present Condition of the Slave
                Population in the Island of Puerto Rico (Philadelphia:
                Adam Waldie, 1832).

1833   Negroes entirely barred from military service.

1834   Publication of important early narrative of George D.
                Flinter, An Account of the Present State of the Island of
                Puerto Rico (London: Longmans, Green 1834).

1836   Over 5 million pounds of cotton were exported. See Coll
                y Toste, op. cit., p. 255.

1837   The Bando de Policía of Governor Lopez de Banos com-
                pelled all landless workers to go to work on local planta-
                tions and to register their names in municipal rolls,
                under penalty of fines.

1839   Birth year of Eugenio Maria de Hostos (1839-1903), noted
                Puerto Rican patriot, writer and educator. In 1939 the
                Government of Puerto Rico published a centenary edition
                of his works (Obras Comletas, 20 vols.; 2nd ed.: San
                Juan: Instituto de Cultura Puertorriqueña, 1970).

1842   Augustin Stahl (1842-1917), great Puerto Rican naturalist, born of German parents in Aguadilla.

1843   Birth year of great Puerto Rican poetess, Lola Rodriguez de Tio, (1843-1924) author of the original hymn, La Borinqueña.

1846   Peak year for slaves in the 19th century when there were 51, 265 slaves out of a total population of 443, 139.

1847-1848   Slave revolt takes place in the north coast town of Vega Baja.

1848   As many as 48 steam mills were in use in the island for the grinding of sugar cane. See Noll Deerr, "The Evolution of the Sugar Cane Mill, Transactions, Newcomen Society for the Study of the History of Engineering and Technology, XXI, London (1943).

              Black Code of General Prim promulgated to discourage slave revolts.

1848-1851   Captain-General Juan de la Pezuela set up a system of work-books which had the effect of regulating labor and turning it into servitude.

1851   The Spanish governor of the island also became vice-patron of the insular church and all salaries and expenses of the church were henceforth assumed by the State. See Coll y Toste, Boletín Historico, VIII, 283-293.

1857   Birth year of José Celso Barbosa, an autonomist and strong advocate of Puerto Rican statehood. Died in 1921.

1859   Birth year of Luis Muñoz Rivera, Puerto Rican patriot and political leader. Died in 1916.

1860   Population had risen to 583, 308 with an overwhelming concentration of labor in agriculture.

1863   Spanish Abolition Society opened an office in Puerto Rico.

1868   On January 2, 1868, Ramón Emeterio Betances, in exile in Santo Domingo, issued a "Provisional Constitution of the Puerto Rican Revolution."

On September 23, patriots in Lares declared a republic,'
but the revolt is quickly squashed.

A law, freeing the children of slaves born after the date
of enactment, was passed.

1870   First indications of formation of political parties on the
            island, reflecting earlier activities of a liberal-reform-
            ist group.

1873   Slavery is abolished.

1874   General Laureano Sanz creates the Civil Guard, essen-
            tially a police instrument against political activity which
            was directed against the government.

1876   Founding of El Ateneo Puertorriqueña which has con-
            tinued to the present as a major force in cultural activi-
            ties in Puerto Rico.

1880   Tobacco production under Spanish rule reaches a peak of
            some 12 million pounds.

1886-1887   United States accounts for 34.99 per cent of Puerto
            Rico's external trade. In 1895-1896 this percentage
            dropped to a low point of less than 18 per cent. By 1899-
            1900, it had climbed to 62.05 per cent.

1887   Autonomists, under Ramón Baldorioty de Castro, ap-
            proved a program calling for an autonomous government.

            Liberal groups on the island adopt a program calling for
            insular self-government.

1888   446 sugar mills were in operation on the island: 286
            driven by oxen, 160 by steam. See Victor S. Clark,
            et al., Porto Rico and Its Problems (Washington: The
            Brookings Institution, 1939).

1891   Pedro Albizu Campos was born on September 12, 1891,
            and became a leading spokesman for the independence of
            Puerto Rico. Died on April 21, 1965.

1897   On November 25, Spain grants autonomy to Puerto Rico.
            Population is 894,302.

1898   The FLT (Federacíon Libre de Trabajadores) is organized, the first trade union of a modern type on the island.

Separation of Church and State put an end to payment of
expenses and salaries of the Catholic church from the insular treasury.

On February 15, the battleship, Maine, blows up in
Havana Harbor; on April 21, the Spanish-American War
begins; on July 25, American troops land at Guánica, on
Puerto Rico's south coast.

1899   Publication of early works by Americans on Puerto Rico,
e.g., William Dinwiddie, Porto Rico: Conditions and
Possibilities (New York: Harper, 1899), an attempt to
appraise business opportunities for mainland entrepren-
eurs; and Albert Gardner Robinson, The Porto Rico of
Today (New York: Scribner, 1899) which sought "To
throw light upon the commercial possibilities in our new
possession that lie within the reach of American business
men."

Report of Commissioner Henry Carroll to President Mc-
Kinley, Report on the Island of Porto Rico (Washington:
Department of War, Government Printing Office, 1899).

On July 1, 1899, General Guy V. Henry organized a system of rural and graded schools, the pupils being
graded so far as possible into six grades, each representing one year's work.

The Treaty of Paris is ratified on April 11, and Spain
cedes Puerto Rico to the United States.

1900   The Foraker Act makes the island a U.S. territory. The
U.S. military government is replaced by a civil administration, headed by an American governor.

1903   Establishment of the University of Puerto Rico by act of
the insular legislature (March 12, 1903) to "provide the
inhabitants of Puerto Rico as soon as possible with the
means of acquiring a thorough knowledge of the various
branches of literature, science and useful arts, including agriculture and mechanical trades, and with professional and technical courses in medicine, law, engineering, pharmacy and in the science and art of teaching."

1904	Formation of Unionist Party, deriving from the Liberal-Reformist Party (1869); the "Assimilationist" Party (1883) and the Autonomist Party (1887).
1917	The Jones Act is passed in Washington on March 2, granting U.S. citizenship to Puerto Ricans.
1918	Death of José de Diego, a campaigner for the Caribbean ideal of a confederation, and the first great orator of the independentista masses.
1922	Balzac v. Porto Rico, 42 S.Ct., 343, 258; U.S. 298, 66 L.Ed. 627 (1922) in which Justice Taft's majority opinion noted that "Puerto Ricans, like Filipinos, were people living in compact and ancient communities, with definitely formed customs and political conceptions ... distant ocean communities of a different origin and language from those of our continental people."
	Nationalist movement is organized by José Coll Cuchi as a breakaway from the Unionist Party.
1923	Juan José Osuna publishes his History of Education in Puerto Rico (Rio Piedras: Editorial de la Universidad de Puerto Rico, 1923; 2nd edition, 1949).
1926	The first scientific analysis of the island's educational needs undertaken: Columbia University Teachers College, Education Survey Commission. See also, Public Education and the Future of Puerto Rico: A Curriculum Survey, 1948-1949 (New York: Bureau of Publications, Teachers College, Columbia University, 1950).
	La Milagrosa, the first church for Puerto Ricans, established by the New York Archdiocese (the church was opened in a converted synagogue on 114th Street and 7th Avenue).
1929	The earliest study of Puerto Ricans in New York City prepared, i.e., Porto Rican Colonies in New York (New York, Urban League, 1929). It was written by William E. Hill.
1930	Dr. José Padín appointed Commissioner of Education by President Herbert Hoover. Dr. Padín believed that Spanish should be the medium of instruction in the elementary school of eight grades, and English the medium of instruction in the high school.

Pedro Albizu Campos is elected President of the militant Nationalist Party.

1934   Transfer of national management of Puerto Rican affairs to Interior Department from Bureau of Insular Affairs of the War Department, where it had been since 1900.

President Roosevelt visits the island and affirms support to rehabilitate the island's economy.

Publication of Antonio S. Pedreira's Insularismo: Ensayos de Interpretacíon Puertorriqueña (San Juan: Bibliotheca de Autores Puertorriqueños).

1935   Five people die in a clash between Nationalists and police at the university.

1936   Two young Nationalists kill insular police chief Riggs and are later killed by the police who arrested them. Albizu Campos and eight followers are jailed for sedition.

1937   Dr. José Gallardo appointed Commissioner of Education by President Franklin D. Roosevelt. Dr. Gallardo modified the Padín policies.

On March 21, nineteen are killed and 100 injured in "the Ponce Massacre," as police open fire on a Nationalist parade.

1938   First comprehensive study of mainland experience of Puerto Rican migrants published: Lawrence Chenault, The Puerto Rican Migrant in New York City (New York: Columbia University Press, 1938; reissued with a new Foreword by F. Cordasco; New York: Russell & Russell, 1970).

Partido Popular Democrático founded by Luis Muñoz Marin.

In July, Nationalists fire at U. S. Governor Winship during a ceremony to mark the fortieth year under American rule. Two Puerto Ri can bodyguards are hit; nine Nationalists are indicted for murder.

1940   Partido Popular Democrático obtains plurality in legislative power.

The new Popular Democratic Party wins the elections. Luis Muñoz Marin becomes Senate President.

Puerto Rican Industrial Development Corporation, an independent government corporation, is empowered to operate plants and assist private enterprise by furnishing credit and tax exemptions for a specified period to new industries. Established by Popular Party.

1941   Rexford Guy Tugwell is named the last U.S. Governor of the island and joins with Muñoz Marín in an ambitious economic development program. See 1942, infra.

1941-1942   Puerto Rico virtually isolated from the mainland by the Nazi submarine command of the Caribbean passages. (See Gordon K. Lewis, Puerto Rico: Freedom and Power in the Caribbean, New York: MR Press, 1963.)

1942   Rexford G. Tugwell becomes Governor of Puerto Rico, the last of the continental governors; served until 1946. See Rexford G. Tugwell, The Stricken Land (New York: Doubleday, 1947), for the problems of colonial administration, the roles of various Puerto Rican leaders during his administration, and the application of Franklin D. Roosevelt's New Deal in Puerto Rico.

1943   Committee on the revision of the Organic Act of Puerto Rico appointed by President Franklin D. Roosevelt. Committee recommended a number of changes in the Federal legislation governing Puerto Rico, including an elected Governor and a judicial advisory council which would be the permanent body concerning itself with Puerto Rican problems.

1944   Popular Party wins the election with 383,000 votes, compared to 208,000 of the combined opposition.

1946   Dr. Mariano Villaronga appointed Commissioner of Education by President Harry S. Truman. Dr. Villaronga made Spanish the medium of instruction in all grades, with English as a required second language, to be taught in special daily classes.

The Partido Independentista Puertorriqueño (PIP) organized at Bayamón on October 20, 1946; later developments include the formation of other pro-independence organizations, e.g., Federacion de Universitarios Pro Independencia (FUPI); and Movimiento Pro Independencia (MPI).

On July 21, President Truman names Jésus T. Piñero as first native Governor of Puerto Rico.

1947   Elective Governor Act provided for election of Governor of Puerto Rico; and for a Coordinator of Federal Agencies with authority for all Federal functions and activities in Puerto Rico.

On August 4, President Truman signs Crawford-Butler Act, permitting Puerto Rico to elect its own governor.

1948   Puerto Rican Department of Labor establishes an office in New York City to serve needs of Puerto Rican migrants to the mainland; in 1949 an office was opened in Chicago; and in 1951 these offices (and others to be opened later) incorporated into the Migration Division, Department of Labor, Commonwealth of Puerto Rico.

Populars win the election, with 392,000 votes against 346,000 of the combined opposition. Luis Muñoz Marín becomes the first popularly elected Governor.

1950   On July 4, President Truman signs Public Law 600, permitting Puerto Rico to draft its own constitution. On October 30, five armed Nationalists attack the Governor's mansion; uprisings erupt in other island towns, causing twenty-seven dead and ninety wounded. On November 1, two New York Puerto Ricans try to kill President Truman; a White House policeman and one assailant die. Albizu Campos and other Nationalists are given long prison sentences for complicity.

1951   On June 4, 387,000 Puerto Ricans favor Public Law 600, 119,000 vote against; over 200,000 registered voters abstain.

Mayor's Committee (New York City) on Puerto Rican Affairs in New York City published Report of the Subcommittee on Education, Recreation and Parks. The report was edited by Leonard Covello, Principal of Benjamin Franklin High School in East Harlem.

1952   On March 3, the new constitution is approved in a referendum, 374,000 to 82,000. On July 25, the Commonwealth Constitution goes into effect, after some changes

insisted upon by Congress, are approved in a second
Puerto Rico referendum. Populars again win the election, with 429,000 votes against a combined opposition
of 232,000. The Independence Party is second with
125,000 votes.

1953   The New York Archdiocese established a special office,
                "The Coordinator of Spanish Catholic Action". It has
                been the function of this office to study the needs of
                Puerto Ricans coming into New York City, and to coor-
                dinate the efforts of the Parishes in providing special
                services.

                High point in migration to the United States' mainland
                achieved with 69,124 Puerto Ricans arriving on the main-
                land.

                The United Nations authorizes the United States to cease
                transmitting information on Puerto Rico as non-self-
                governing territory.

1953-1957   The New York City Board of Education sponsors The
                Puerto Rican Study which addressed itself to two major
                problems: teaching English as a second language to
                Puerto Rican pupils, and identifying techniques to pro-
                mote a more rapid and effective adjustment of Puerto
                Rican parents and children to the community, and the
                community to them. See The Puerto Rican Study (New
                York City: Board of Education, 1958; reissued 1972).

1954   On March 1, four Nationalists open fire in the U.S.
                House of Representatives, wounding five Congressmen.

1955   Founding of the Instituto de Cultura Puertorriqueña as
                an independent public corporation whose purpose is to
                study and preserve the national historical and cultural
                heritage and to foster and propagate all forms of Puerto
                Rican culture.

1955-1956   Puerto Rican Forum established by a group of Puerto
                Rican intellectuals to promote the interests of Puerto
                Ricans in New York City. Its Executive Director (1973)
                is Hector Vazquez.

1956   The Chicago Archdiocese established the "Bishop's Com-
                mittee for the Spanish Speaking in Chicago" which ad-
                dresses itself to the needs of Mexican-Americans and
                Puerto Ricans.

Populars win the election with 62 per cent of the total
vote. The Statehood Republican Party doubles its 1952
total with 172,000 votes; the Independence Party drops to
85,000.

1957   Institute of Intercultural Communication founded at the
Catholic University (Ponce, Puerto Rico) by Ivan Illich
and sponsored by Francis Cardinal Spellman. The institute prepares priests, religious personnel and lay people
to work with Puerto Ricans on the mainland.

1958   Elena Padilla publishes Up from Puerto Rico, a cultural
anthropological study of Puerto Rican migrants in New
York City.

1959   Founding of the Academia de Artes y Ciencias de Puerto
Rico which has promoted the arts and sciences in Puerto
Rico. In 1967, the Academia instituted an annual pro-
gram of awards.

Congress rejects the Fernos-Murray Bill, which aimed
to amplify Puerto Rico's autonomy.

1960   Life expectancy in Puerto Rico fixed at 70 years; it had
been 38 years in 1910.

Populars win the election with 59 per cent of the 800,000
votes. The Statehooders are second, and the Independence Party drops to only 3 per cent.

1961   Aspira founded in New York City by the Puerto Rican
Forum to promote higher education opportunities for
Puerto Ricans. Louis Nuñez, President of Aspira, states
its goal: "To channel the rising aspirations of our youth,
especially those in college, into orderly, systematic programs for community development."

Jésus Colon published A Puerto Rican in New York and
other Sketches.

1962   Herman Badillo (born 1929 in Caguas, Puerto Rico) is
named Commissioner of the Office of Relocation (New
York City). He was elected Borough President of the
Bronx (New York City) in 1965; and in 1970 won election
to the House of Representatives. He is the first elected
Puerto Rican Congressman.

René Marqués published El Puertorriqueño Docil, an
interpretation of the failure of the nationalist movement
of the 1950s.

1963   The Puerto Rican Family Institute established in New
York City as a Puerto Rican effort in the area of professional social service, largely as the effort of Augustino Gonzales assisted by a team of volunteers. In 1965
the Institute was given support by the New York City
Council Against Poverty and was made a citywide agency.

1964   The Puerto Rican Forum articulates The Puerto Rican
Community Development Project (Un Projecto Puertorriqueño De Ayuda Mutua), a comprehensive development for the Puerto Rican Community. The position
paper was prepared by Professor Frank Bonilla, a member of the faculty of the Massachusetts Institute of Technology. The proposed program recommended promoting
a sense of identity among Puerto Ricans in New York City
which would help them develop community strength.

The Status Commission begins to study the island's political status. Muñoz Marín retires from the governorship; his handpicked successor, Roberto Sánchez Vilella,
becomes the Popular candidate and easily wins the election.

1965   The Civil Rights Act (1965) abolishes literacy tests in
English as a prerequisite to registering to vote. Puerto
Ricans not literate in English may now register by simply
showing evidence of having completed 6 years of schooling in Puerto Rico.

1966   Two days of rioting in the Chicago Puerto Rican Community (June 13, 14) followed a policeman shooting a
Puerto Rican youth. As a consequence, a Puerto Rican
was appointed to the Mayor's committee on Human Relations. Riots have marked the lives of Puerto Ricans in
Jersey City, New Jersey (June 1970); Paterson, New Jersey (July 1968); Passaic, New Jersey (August 1969); Perth
Amboy, New Jersey (August 1966); and Trenton, New
Jersey (June 1969).

Senator Robert F. Kennedy honored by Society of Friends
of Puerto Rico (May 13, 1966).

Mayor John Lindsay appoints Teodoro Moscoso special
consultant on Puerto Rican Community affairs and economic development.

1967   Elfren Ramirez, who founded a successful rehabilitation
program for drug addicts in Puerto Rico, was brought to
New York City by Mayor John Lindsay to establish a
similar program.

The first New York City Conference of the Puerto Rican
Community is convened (April) and submits recommendations to the Mayor. See Puerto Ricans Confront Problems
of the Complex Urban Society: A Design for Change
(1968).

Publication of Piri Thomas' Down These Mean Streets,
a moving autobiography of a black Puerto Rican growing
up in the East Harlem (New York City) barrio.

The first study of migration back to the island from the
United States was published by José Hernandez Alvarez,
Return Migration to Puerto Rico (Berkeley: University of
California Press, 1967).

Over 5,000 demonstrate for independence on April 16th
in San Juan, during fete marking 101st anniversary of
birth of patriot, José de Diego.

On July 23, in status referendum, Commonwealth wins
60.5 per cent of the votes, compared with 38.9 per cent
for statehood and .6 per cent for independence. Ad hoc
committees are to be formed to work out the perfection
of the commonwealth status.

1968   Manuel Casiano, Puerto Rican Civic leader, appointed
Director, Migration Division, Department of Labor,
Commonwealth of Puerto Rico. See 1948. Succeeded in
that office by Nick Lugo, who is the current Director
(1973).

In May 1968, Aspira conducted a nationwide conference
in New York City on the "special educational needs of
Puerto Rican youth," and published a report, Hemos
Trabajado Bien.

Roberto Garcia won election to the New York State Senate.
In the same legislative session, Garcia was joined in the
Assembly by three Puerto Ricans elected to state office:
Armando Montano, Luis Nine and Manuel Ramos.

A Ford Foundation grant makes possible the formation
of Aspira affiliates in other cities of high Puerto Rican
population - Chicago, Philadelphia, Newark and San Juan.
See 1961.

A rift in the Popular Party causes Sánchez Vilella to
leave and he forms his own People's Party. Luis Negrón
Lopez is the Popular candidate. Luis A. Ferré and the
pro-statehood New Progressive Party win by a narrow
margin, interrupting twenty-eight years of Popular Party
rule.

Governor Nelson Rockefeller proclaims New York State
day (July 21) honoring Luis Muñoz Rivera, who led fight
for United States' citizenship for Puerto Ricans.

1968-1969   Evelina Antonetti founded and guides the United Bronx
Parents (New York City) which carries on a vigorous
campaign for the improvement of the schools in poor
areas.

Joseph Monserrat, former Director of the Migration Division, Commonwealth of Puerto Rico, appointed a member (and first President) of the interim Board of Education of New York City. During the 1960s, Joseph Monserrat headed the Migration Division, Department of
Labor, Commonwealth of Puerto Rico, which provided a
wide range of services to Puerto Ricans on the mainland.

1969   Miriam Colón established the Puerto Rican Traveling
Theatre in New York City, which tours the streets in
summertime, presenting Puerto Rican dramas to the
people of the neighborhoods.

Marta Valle is appointed New York City Commissioner
of the Youth Services Agency by Mayor John Lindsay.
Other appointments by Mayor John Lindsay included
Amalia Bentanzos as Commissioner of Relocation, and
Joseph Rodriquez Erazo as Commissioner of Manpower
and Career Development.

Aspira extends educational counseling to 4,909 Aspir-
antes, with 2,297 youngsters enrolled as members of
Aspira leadership Clubs. See 1961.

New York State Human Rights Division report puts number of Puerto Rican residents in state at 1,020,900, up
378,300 (59%) since 1960; maintains that 969,700 live in
New York City but that largest increases were recorded
in other areas of state.

Puerto Rican Planning Board reported that migration to
the United States dropped sharply in 1969 with 7,000 more
persons coming to the island than leaving.

A special drive undertaken to register Puerto Rican
voters in New York City. The Citizens Voter Registration Campaign estimated that 131,000 Puerto Ricans were
registered in New York City out of a potential voting body
of 435,000.

Puerto Rican students take a large part in demonstrations
which shut down City College (City University of New
York), and in militant actions at other divisions of the
university (Queens, Brooklyn, Lehman Colleges) which
result in the establishment of Puerto Rican studies programs.

Young Lords Party, founded in New York City as an action group of young Puerto Ricans concerned with health
and related social needs of the Puerto Rican Community.
An independent branch operates in Chicago. Its leaders
have included José Jiminez, Omar Lopez, Milo Villa-
gomez, Alberto Chivera, Felipe Luciano and David Perez.

1970   Puerto Ricans in New Jersey organized a statewide Puerto
Rican Conference, as a basis of political power and influence. A leading figure in the Conference was Dr.
Hilda Hidalgo, a professor at Livington College, Rut-
gers - the State University of New Jersey.

Eugenio Maria de Hostos Community College (City University of New York) is established, largely to serve the
needs of the Puerto Rican Community in which it is lo-
cated. Cándido de Leon became its president in 1971.

Migration from Puerto Rico to the mainland falls to 1,811 persons as a result of the mainland recession. The net exodus since 1940 from the island has been 800,000.

El Museo del Barrio, New York City's first museum of Puerto Rican culture moves into a new headquarters at Public School 125, West 123rd Street. Director Robert Ortiz says museum seeks to help Puerto Ricans develop cultural identity and sense of pride in their community; programs are intended not only to reflect El Barrio, the Puerto Rican ghetto in East Harlem, but all mainland Puerto Rican communities.

Governor Ferré and President Nixon form an ad hoc committee to discuss the U. S. presidential vote for Puerto Rico. Muñoz Marín retires from the Senate.

MIRA, Puerto Rican revolutionary and pro-independence group, acknowledges carrying out 19 terrorist acts since December 1969, including 7 in New York City; and pledges to continue attacks. See New York Times, February 13, 1970.

1971   American Museum of Natural History, New York City, presents exhibit on Puerto Rican contemporary life. See New York Times, March 3, 1971.

Mayor John Lindsay proclaims week of June 7th, Puerto Rican Cultural Week.

New York City Puerto Ricans celebrate founding of Puerto Rico Discovery Day with series of events in schools, churches and community centers. See New York Times, November 19, 1971.

Spanish-surnamed Congressmen announce sponsorship of National Conference of Mexican-American and Puerto Rican groups to discuss lack of justice over last decade. See New York Times, September 26, 1971.

United States issues stamp, commemorating San Juan's 450th anniversary.

Cuban representative to the United Nations proposes resolution to have United States Colonialism in Puerto Rico debated during meeting of United Nations Trusteeship Council. See New York Times, September 24, 1971.

1972   Roberto Clemente of Pittsburgh Pirates (the 11th man in
                major league history to reach 3,000 hit plateau) dies
                in plane crash off Puerto Rico while flying in supplies to
                Managua, Nicaragua, leveled by earthquake.

                Commerce Department reports number of Puerto Ricans
                in United States rose by 55% over last decade; reports
                population in 1970 was 1,379,043 with 63% of Puerto
                Ricans living in New York State; New Jersey and Illinois
                reported as having second and third next largest Puerto
                Rican populations.

                The Puerto Rican Research and Resources Center opened
                in Washington, D.C. to serve as a general research re-
                source on island/mainland experience. Antonia Pantoja
                named director, with members of the Board of Directors,
                including Blanca Cedena, Hilda Hidalgo, Victor Rivera,
                José Moscoso and Francisco Trilla.

                Popular Democratic Party is returned to power with the
                election of Rafael Hernandez Colón as the new Governor.

                Hernan La Fontaine appointed director of New York City
                Office of Bi-lingual Education by Board of Education. The
                office of Bi-lingual Education, operating on a citywide
                basis, to meet the needs of non-English-speaking chil-
                dren (predominantly Puerto Rican) was recommended by
                a Bi-lingual Commission convened by Chancellor of Edu-
                cation, Harvey Scribner, and chaired by Professor Julio
                Morales.

                The preliminary 1970 Federal census reports, reporting
                811,834 Puerto Ricans in New York City, were challenged
                by Nick Lugo, Director of the Migration Division, Com-
                monwealth of Puerto Rico, who estimated that there
                were 1.2 million Puerto Ricans in the city. See New York
                Times, April 20, 1972.

1973   On February 2, 1973, Pope Paul VI elevates Luis Aponte
                Martinez, Bishop of San Juan, to the College of Cardinals.

DOCUMENTS

Legal-Constitutional Factors in Relation to the Status of Puerto Rico *

A. HISTORICAL BACKGROUND

1. Relationship with Spain: 1493–1898

For 300 years, following the discovery of Puerto Rico by Christopher Columbus in 1493, Spain treated Puerto Rico as a military outpost in the Western Hemisphere. The system of government established for Puerto Rico and for the other Spanish colonies in the New World was derived from the Code of Laws of the Indies (1691) and the revised Code of Spanish Laws (1795) both of which followed the doctrine of royal absolutism.[1]

This principle when extended to Puerto Rico meant that prior to the 19th century power was centered in a virtually omnipotent Governor who not only was the chief executive but also promulgated decrees, headed the army and navy, was the chief fiscal official, the supreme judge and, as royal vice-patron, participated also in ecclesiastical authority. This total concentration of power in one official was coupled with a high degree of governmental control over human affairs. Thus, after a series of encounters, the Indian population was subjugated and even for the Spanish white colonists movement from town to town required express permission.[2]

In the 19th century there was a major growth in population in Puerto Rico from about 150,000 people in 1800 to a million people by the end of the century.[3] This rapid rise was in part the result of the influx of Spanish royalists who fled the revolutions against the mother country which swept Central and South America. Its immediate significance was that it changed the balance in Puerto Rico between the Negro-Indian population and the Spanish population in favor of the Spanish.[4]

This burgeoning of the politically aware population gave rise to serious agitation by Puerto Ricans for increased participation in their own government. Partly as a consequence of political difficulties for Spain in

[1] Monclova, "The Puerto Rican Political Movement in the XIX Century" (STACOM Special Study 1966) pp. 13–14.
[2] Ibid., pp. 6–10, 14.
[3] U.S. Census Bureau, vol. I, pt. 53, pp. 53–59, table 1. The exact statistics given are: In 1800, 155,426; 1899, 953,243.
[4] Lewis, "Puerto Rico: Freedom and Power in the Caribbean" (1963), p. 58.

* Report of the United States–Puerto Rico Commission on the Status of Puerto Rico (Washington: Government Printing Office, 1966), pp. 31–48.

Europe, Spain during the first quarter of the 19th century made its first major political concession to Puerto Rico. On July 14, 1812, Governor Meléndez Bruna promulgated a circular which declared the Spanish National Constitution effective in Puerto Rico. This Constitution, the first of its kind to be approved in Spain, declared Puerto Rico an integral part of the monarchy. It granted Spanish citizenship to all free native-born Puerto Ricans and confirmed the right to name a deputy with a voice and a vote in the Spanish Cortes (the Spanish Parliament). In addition, it created a municipal corporation called a provincial assembly, composed of nine members: the Governor, the intendent, and seven landholders. This Provincial Assembly had limited powers over certain local activities.

During the rest of the century, the population of Puerto Rico continued to grow and to agitate for greater home rule. At various times reforms were promised by Spain but always Puerto Rican hopes were frustrated. In 1896 an agreement with the Spanish Liberal Party was effected by Puerto Rico's leaders so that when this party came to power later that year, it arranged for the declaration of an autonomous charter for the island.[5]

Before 1897, pursuant to the Spanish National Constitution, the government of Puerto Rico was headed by a Governor General appointed by the Crown possessing broad executive and military powers. Islanders were at times members of the Cortes but their influence was not very great. Laws were either enacted in Spain or decreed by the Spanish appointed executive officials. Some municipal self-government was provided, but its effectiveness was often negated when Governors virtually handpicked candidates for local office. The number of persons permitted to vote and serve in public office was sharply limited by rigid educational and property qualifications. In short, for most of the period of Spanish rule, opportunities for political expression and for a voice in the affairs of government were negligible for the vast majority of the people of Puerto Rico.[6]

The Charter of 1897 was a substantial improvement upon this state of affairs. Puerto Rico would now elect delegates with full voting rights to both houses of the Cortes. In addition, there was established an elected Chamber of Representatives on the island and a 15-man Council of Administration (Senate), 8 of whom were elected by Puerto Rico. The Governor General would continue to be appointed by the crown and would select the remaining seven Councillors. The powers of the Governor were reduced by the initiatives allowed to the Puerto Rican Legislature, but he retained the right to suspend civil rights and to refer insular legislation to the Council of Ministers of Spain if he felt it to be detrimental or unconstitutional. The Puerto Rican Legislature was generally given power to pass on all matters of purely insular importance: to fix the budget and determine tariffs and

[5] "Constitution Establishing Self-Government in the Island of Puerto Rico by Spain in 1897," in Documents on the Constitutional History of Puerto Rico, 2d ed., revised (Washington : Office of the Commonwealth of Puerto Rico, 1964), p. 22.

[6] Hunter, "Historical Survey of the Puerto Rico Status Question" (STACOM Special Study 1965), p. 3.

taxes.[7] Commercial treaties were to be concluded by the home government but provision was made for Puerto Rican Government concurrence.[8]

The Charter of Autonomy was stated to be bilateral in character.[9] However, the powers of the Governor General were exceedingly broad [10] so that precise participation of the Puerto Rican people in their own government is unclear.

The Charter of Autonomy was decreed in November 1897. In February 1898, the first Puerto Rican cabinet was appointed and, in March, general elections were held for the legislature. In April the Spanish-American War was declared and in July 1898, American troops occupied Puerto Rico. The Charter of Autonomy was, thus, in actual operation for a very short time. How well the Charter of Autonomy would have worked out in practice no one can say. On paper it granted Puerto Rico a greater degree of self-government than Puerto Rico was to receive under the Foraker Act of 1900, although substantially less than Puerto Rico has today.

The above history is significant for the perspective it gives to subsequent Puerto Rico-United States relations. Although the problem of United States-Puerto Rico relations was completely novel to mainland officials, to Puerto Rican leaders the issues appeared much the same as under the Spanish. The failure for many years of continental leaders to recognize that what to the United States was the beginning of a dialog was to Puerto Rico the interruption of a long and continuous effort at the moment when it seemed finally to be successful contributed to many ill-considered and deprecatory statements by mainland leaders. Much of the impatience of Puerto Rican leaders in the early 1900's represented the accumulation of frustration and resentment acquired through many years of struggle in their quest for self-government. On the other hand, the heritage of frustration was to make portions of the Puerto Rican populace less receptive and very skeptical of significant attitudinal and institutional changes when they occurred.

2. Relationship With the United States: 1898–1950

The Spanish-American War and the Treaty of Paris, which concluded it, brought a new series of problems to the United States. For the first time— Hawaii also had just been acquired—the United States was in charge of governing territories which were geographically separated from the mainland with large numbers of people culturally quite distant from the culture of North America.

These problems were immediately recognized and the best way to solve them was the subject of lengthy debates both in Congress, the executive branch, and in the 1900 presidential campaign. The debates centered about the shorthand question: whether the Constitution followed the flag. Legally what was at issue was: (1) whether the inhabitants of the newly acquired territories, including Puerto Rico, were automatically citizens of the United States; (2) whether the inhabitants of the newly acquired territories,

---

[7] Art. 35 ; but see art. 36.
[8] Art. 37.
[9] Art. 2 of Additional Articles ; Preamble, *passium*.
[10] E.g., art. 2, 3, 41–43, 51.

including Puerto Rico, had the protection of the Bill of Rights vis-a-vis the Federal Government; and (3) whether the Constitution prevented the imposition of tariffs on imports from these territories. In 1900 Congress answered each of these questions in the negative.

The Foraker Act which Congress passed in 1900 established a temporary civil government for Puerto Rico in place of the military occupation. The Senate report which accompanied the act expressed the desire to permit Puerto Rico's participation in government and to avoid as far as possible radical changes in the Spanish code and judicial procedure then governing Puerto Rico. The report went on to indicate the problems arising from the hurricane of August 8, 1899, the widespread illiteracy, and the lack of a general system of public education.[11]

Under the Foraker Act, executive authority was vested in the Governor and an 11-member executive council, 5 of whom were to be Puerto Ricans, all appointed by the President. This council also constituted the upper chamber of the legislature and six of its members were to hold high executive positions. The lower house of delegates was to be composed of 35 members elected biannually by all who qualified as voters on March 1, 1900.

The Governor could veto laws passed by the legislature, but his veto could be overridden by a two-thirds majority of the insular legislature. Congress, however, reserved to itself the absolute authority to annul any law passed by the Puerto Rican Legislature. Congress never exercised this power.

An insular Supreme Court was established (appointed by the President) with an appeal directly from it to the U.S. Supreme Court. In addition, a U.S. district court in Puerto Rico was also established. Finally, the act provided for a resident Commissioner to be elected biannually who would represent Puerto Rico in Congress.

The Foraker Act disappointed Puerto Rico's leaders. They had expected the democratic United States, in contrast to monarchist Spain, to be more rather than less respectful of local government. On March 2, 1917, a new Organic Act, known as the Jones Act, was passed which was primarily designed to increase Puerto Rico's participation in its own government and to eliminate, to a degree, the distinction made by the Foraker Act and approved in the insular cases between the citizens of the United States and the citizens of Puerto Rico.

Thus, the upper house which had been appointed by the President was, under the Jones Act, to be elected, and the majority of the department heads were now to be appointed by the Governor with the advice and consent of the insular Senate. The Governor similarly was to appoint the insular magistrates with the advice and consent of the insular Senate. This transfer of power from Congress and Federal Government to the local officials was not complete since the Attorney General, the Commissioner of Education, and the Auditor were still appointed by the President as were the members of the Puerto Rico Supreme Court.

Most significantly, the 1917 legislation reversed the decision that had been

---

taken in 1900 and offered U.S. citizenship to Puerto Rico, with the option of refusal in individual cases, and promulgated a bill of rights for the island.

In the following decades Puerto Rico urged increased control of its own affairs. On March 8, 1943, President Franklin Delano Roosevelt appointed a committee on the revision of the Organic Act of Puerto Rico composed of Secretary Harold Ickes; Abe Fortas, Under Secretary of the Interior; Rexford Tugwell, then Governor of Puerto Rico; Father Raymond A. Mc-Gowan; Senator Luis Muñoz Marín, then president of the Puerto Rican Senate and chairman of the Popular Democratic Party; Martín Travieso, chief justice of the Puerto Rican Supreme Court; Senator Celestino Iriarte, chairman of the Union Republican Party; and Jose Ramírez-Santibánez, chairman of the Liberal Party.

The Committee recommended a number of changes in the Federal legislation governing Puerto Rico, including an elected Governor and a judicial advisory council which would be the permanent body concerning itself with Puerto Rican problems. The bill suggested by the Committee did not pass. It was not until 1947 in the Elective Governor Act that Puerto Rico obtained an elected Governor. The Governor was given the power to appoint, with the advice and consent of the insular Senate, the heads of all executive departments. In addition, the 1947 act provided for a Coordinator of Federal Agencies, a Federal official who was given authority over all Federal functions and activities in Puerto Rico. Finally, the President was given the authority to exempt Puerto Rico from Federal laws not specifically made applicable to Puerto Rico by Congress.

At this stage, prior to 1950, Congress still reserved to itself the power to nullify all insular legislation and the President continued to have the power of final veto over insular laws. As mentioned earlier, Congress had never exercised its power of nullification and in only three cases had the President exercised his power in upholding the Governor's veto.[12]

B. THE PRESENT LEGAL RELATIONSHIP BETWEEN PUERTO RICO AND THE UNITED STATES

1. The Legislation of 1950–52

In 1950, the U.S. Congress passed Public Law 600 [13] which stated:

". . . fully recognizing the principle of government by consent . . .
the people of Puerto Rico may organize a government pursuant to a

---

[12] In 1946, Governor Tugwell vetoed three bills which were passed over his veto by the Puerto Rican Legislature and were consequently submitted to the President who upheld the Governor. One of the bills provided for the use of Spanish as the language of instruction in public schools, another for a plebiscite in which the people of the island would express their preference for independence, statehood, or dominion status, and the third provided a poll amongst qualified voters in each of the popular parties which would submit the names of its candidates for officer of Governor. Governor Tugwell had vetoed the bills on the ground that they related to the island's ultimate status. "46th Annual Report of the Governor of Puerto Rico, 1946," pp. 4–5 ; White House press releases of May 18 and Oct. 26, 1946.

[13] 64 Stat. 319, July 3, 1950.

constitution of their own adoption." This law was adopted "in the nature of a compact."

The act provided it become effective only after a referendum held in accordance with the laws of Puerto Rico. This referendum was limited to approval or disapproval of Public Law 600. If approved by a majority of the voters participating in the referendum, the Puerto Rican Legislature could call a constitutional convention to draft a constitution. If this constitution were approved by the people of Puerto Rico, it should be submitted via the President to Congress for its approval. In addition, Public Law 600 repealed portions of the Jones Act of 1917, the basic Federal law governing Puerto Rico, and renamed the remainder the Puerto Rican Federal Relations Act.

The people of Puerto Rico did vote and approved the law. A constitution was drafted, approved, and submitted to Congress which, in Public Law 447,[14] approved it conditional upon the following changes: (1) deletion of a provision patterned after the United Nations Universal Declaration of Human Rights recognizing the right to work, obtain an adequate standard of living, and social protection in old age or sickness; (2) addition of a provision assuring continuance of private elementary schools; and (3) addition of a provision requiring that amendment to the Puerto Rico Constitution must be consistent with the U.S. Constitution, the Puerto Rican Federal Relations Act, and Public Law 600. All three changes required by the Congress were made by Puerto Rico and approved by the Puerto Rican Constitutional Convention and later by another referendum.

It should be noted that this legal activity in 1950–52 was undertaken with the maximum degree of formality and ceremonial solemnity in both Puerto Rico and the United States. Officials both in Puerto Rico and in the United States were aware that what was taking place was a significant alteration in the relationships between Puerto Rico and the United States.[15] This information was clearly transmitted to the Puerto Rican people in the debates and referendums during this period. All of the major parties and political leaders in Puerto Rico analyzed, argued, discussed, and urged a position on the new constitution and the Commonwealth.

When the time came to draft the constitution, the Puerto Rican people went to considerable length to obtain the best talent available to assist them in drafting it. The list of consultants from the mainland and elsewhere who were asked to bring to bear their abilities in drafting a new constitution for Puerto Rico included some of the leading constitutional lawyers and theorists in the world. There is at least one excellent book of commentaries which considers in depth the many issues with which the Puerto Ricans concerned themselves.[16]

---

[14] 66 Stat. 327, July 3, 1952.

[15] This was partly reflected in the fact that in Puerto Rico the process of approving the constitution was attended by violence from Oct. 30–Nov. 6, 1950, in various parts of the island, resulting in approximately 28 persons killed and 49 wounded. The Nationalist Party, a small minority of the population advocating independence, also stimulated violence on the mainland which resulted in the attempted assassination of President Truman on Nov. 1, 1950.

[16] University of Puerto Rico, School of Public Administration, "La Nueva Constitución de Puerto Rico" (1954).

Similarly, the debates both in Congress [17] and in Puerto Rico [18] explored at great length the consequences of this procedure and the formation of a Puerto Rican Government under its own constitution. Hypothetical legal questions were posed which reached into the farthest corners of international and constitutional law where no one could speak with sureness and time was the only factor which could determine the problem with certainty. For example, many questioned the division of power between Puerto Rico and the Federal Government under commonwealth comparing it with statehood. To some it seemed that under statehood this allocation of power was clear and under commonwealth it was uncertain.

The fact is, however, that the problems of Federal-State power allocation have been evolving since the time of the founding of the Republic and recent years have indicated the uncertainty and instability from a legal point of view in many areas of this relationship. In short, a Federal relationship—whether it be commonwealth or statehood—is never completely clear. Rather there is a necessary and desirable obscure fringe area which permits many legal, political, and practical adjustments to take place. It is true that Commonwealth has many areas of uncertainty because it is novel. But it is also true that commonwealth like statehood has many areas of uncertainty because of the nature of a Federal relationship.

These questions as to the precise legal consequences under various hypothetical circumstances arose only because of the agreement, both in the Congress and in Puerto Rico, that an extraordinary event which was going to transform the Puerto Rico-mainland relationship was then taking place. To note just a few of these changes is to indicate the magnitude of that which has occurred. Thus, Puerto Rico now elects its own Governor, elects its own legislature, appoints its own judges, appoints all its cabinet officials and all other lesser officials in its executive branch, sets its own educational policies, determines its own budget, and amends its own civil and criminal code. All of this is done without participation by, concurrence of, or even information submitted to, any Federal officials. No one in the Puerto Rican or Federal Government, either in the legislative or executive branch, has indicated that these conditions should change and that what has in fact occurred should not continue to be the situation. No one in the Puerto Rican or the Federal Government has suggested that power granted to Puerto Rico in 1950–52 should be diminished or subordinated or that there should be a return to the previously existing situation.

The legal problems then arise in a situation where doctrinal argumenta-

---

[17] The congressional hearings and debates are reported in House of Representatives, Hearings Before the Committee on Public Lands on H.R. 7674 and S. 3336 (July 12, 1949, Mar. 14, May 16, June 8, 1950) (81st Cong. 2d sess.) ; House of Representatives, Hearings Before the Committee on Interior and Insular Affairs on H.J. Res. 430 (Apr. 25, 1952) (82d Cong. 2d sess.) ; U.S. Senate, Hearings Before a Subcommittee of the Committee on Interior and Insular Affairs on S. 3336 (May 17, 1950) (81st Cong., 2d sess.) ; U.S. Senate, Hearings Before the Committee on Interior and Insular Affairs on S.J. Res. 151 (Apr. 29, May 6, 1952) (82d Cong., 2d sess.) ; and the 96th and 98th volumes of the Congressional Record, *passim*.

[18] Commonwealth of Puerto Rico, "Diario de Sesiones de la Convención Constituyente de Puerto Rico" (4 vols., 1961 ed.), *passim*.

tion rather than practical concern calls most loudly for their immediate resolution. It is the practical problems which arise, however, which will effect their ultimate resolution. This will take place gradually as the executive, judicial, and legislative branches of both the Federal and Puerto Rican Governments continue to act, to discuss, and to respond to problems as they arise.

What then are the legal issues which are of primary concern between Puerto Rico and the United States at present which will require resolution? The one which has been most debated in Puerto Rico is the issue of the compact: the question of whether the 1950–52 legislation resulted in a relationship which could not be changed without the consent of either party.

The legal issue of the compact may be analyzed as follows:

1. Does Congress have the power to enter into such a compact with Puerto Rico?
2. Assuming arguendo, it did have the power, did Congress exercise this power when it passed Public Law 600, and, if so, what are the terms of the agreement?

Since these issues have been so frequently discussed, at times rather confusingly, perhaps it would be well at this point to explore briefly the legal arguments with respect to these questions.

1. Does Congress have the power to enter into such a compact with Puerto Rico?

The sources of congressional power with respect to territories derive from (a) the territorial clause of the Constitution, article IV, section 3, clause 2, which states: "The Congress shall have power to dispose of and make all needful rules and regulations respecting the Territory or other property belonging to the United States . . ." and (b) the inherent and implied powers of the National Government.[19]

The argument in favor of compact is that the power stemming from both of these sources is extremely broad and includes the power to make contracts with territories. Compact advocates cite cases where the U.S. Congress has contracted with its citizens [20] and even with its territories, most notably with the Territory of Minnesota,[21] the Territory of Wisconsin,[22] and the Northwest Territory.[23]

---

[19] With respect to Puerto Rico, the issue may also be affected by the Treaty of Paris.

[20] *Perry* v. *United States*, 294 U.S. 330 (1935). (Congress could not change obligation imposed by gold clause in U.S. Government bonds. Although obligation upheld, citizen did not prove damage and, therefore, accorded no remedy.) *Lynch* v. *United States*, 292 U.S. 571 (1934). (Congress could not abrogate war risk insurance contracts authorized by previous Congress and already entered into.)

[21] *Stearns* v. *Minnesota*, 179 U.S. 223 (1900). (Court held Minnesota could not tax railroad land other than on gross receipts because it would impair contract with railroad created by prior State legislation and would violate compact entered between United States and Minnesota created by Enabling Act and constitution of the States.)

[22] *Beecher* v. *Wetherby*, 95 U.S. 517 (1877). (Court held title to given land in defendant since defendant obtained land from State. The State had received it by virtue of compact entered into between United States and Wisconsin created by Enabling Act and admission statute passed by Congress. Congressional attempt to subsequently dispose of land, therefore, invalid.)

[23] Sec. 14, Ordinance of 1787; *Pollard* v. *Kibbe*, 39 U.S. (14 Pet.) 351, 417–418 (1840). (After treaty with Spain but before United States gained possession, Spanish Governor

The opponents of compact agree that the sources of congressional power arise from the territorial clause of the Constitution and the implied powers of the National Government, both of which are quite broad in scope. This very breadth, however, they state, permits the Congress at any time to modify legislation previously adopted for a territory. They argue, citing cases, that although Congress may delegate powers to a territorial government, the broad powers granted to Congress under the Constitution remain and may be exercised should the need arise.[24] They distinguish the cases cited by compact supporters noted above, stating they treat of proprietary rather than political rights.

The examination of this problem has been very careful. Extensive hearings have been held in Puerto Rico in which the views of the most eminent members of the Puerto Rica Bar were heard on this issue. For example, the Puerto Rico Bar Association in its own examination of the question indicated the difficulty of a certain response and argued that the solution revolved around the problem of sovereignty, which either totally or partially should be transferred to Puerto Rico.[25] The Puerto Rico Anti-Colonialist Congress similarly analyzed the legal problem in term of sovereignty, emphasizing the continued exercise of various powers by the Federal Government which they felt prevented a meaningful bilateral relationship with the terms of the United Nations definition.[26] Others were less concerned with the issue of sovereignty and discussed specific aspects of commonwealth which indicated a bilateral relationship.[27] In addition, the Status Commission had the benefit of a Legal Consultative Committee, composed of leading lawyers and academicians in both Puerto Rico and the mainland who addressed themselves to these problems.

The conclusion reached is that the national government has the power to provide to its citizens a form of government and a participation in its own affairs in accordance with their desires. The entire history of the United States-territorial relationship and the Federal Government-citizen relationship sustain innovation and change in accordance with needs. We can see no constitutional bar to prevent Congress under the existing Con-

---

transferred land to Pollard contrary to previous transfer, prior to treaty, by Spanish Government to Forbes & Co. Congress said to have confirmed transfer to Pollard. Court referred to Northwest Ordinance as solemn and mutual compact under which Congress could authorize title in Pollard.) ; *Scott* v. *Detroit Young Men's Society Lessee*, 1 Doug. 119 (Mich. 1843). (Prior to formal admission as a State but after organization pursuant to the Northwest Ordinance, Michigan authorities granted in the name of the State an association charter. Court held this grant valid since people of Michigan had right to organize as State pursuant to the Northwest Ordinance.) ; The Ordinance of 1787 is discussed extensively noting cases which would tend to support and reject the compact thesis in Haight, *The Ordinance of 1787*, 2 Mich. Pol. Sci. Ass'n. 343 (1897).

[24] *National Bank* v. *County of Yankton*, 101 U.S. 129, 133 (1879). (Bonds issued by territory of Dakota held valid because of act of Congress which has power to repeal, modify, or validate act of territorial legislature.) ; *Murphy* v. *Ramsey*, 114 U.S. 15, 44 (1885). (Court upheld act of Congress abridging right to vote of those practicing polygamy in Territory of Utah even though contrary to territorial legislation.)

[25] STACOM hearings, testimony of the Puerto Rico Bar Association, May 14, 1965.

[26] STACOM hearings, testimony of the Puerto Rico Anti-Colonialist Congress, May 15, 1965.

[27] STACOM hearings, e.g., testimony of Enrique Bird Piñero, May 17, 1965.

stitution of the United States from entering into innovative forms of relationships within the Federal structure—including a binding relationship—in order to meet the needs and desires of the Puerto Rican people.

2. *Assuming arguendo, it did have the power, did Congress exercise this power when it passed Public Law 600 and, if so, what are the terms of the agreement?*

Advocates of compact rely primarily on (a) the words of the statute, (b) the procedure required by the statute, and (c) the subsequent actions by the executive branch before the United Nations and the Congress in certain instances.

If Congress intended nothing but another Organic Act why did it say "in the nature of a compact" in Public Law 600, and, in the preamble to Public Law 447, refer to Public Law 600 as a compact? In addition, the procedure set up by Public Law 600—a referendum, the drafting of the constitution, another referendum in Puerto Rico, and subsequent approval by Congress of the constitution—is similar to the procedure often followed when territories become States or, as in the case of the Philippines, become independent. In those cases Congress frequently used the word "compact," as it did here, and indicated that the conditions imposed by Congress permitting the territory to draft the constitution are binding in both the territory and the National Government. Thus, the advocates of compact argue, the language of the statute and the procedure adopted were associated in the congressional mind with a permanent change of status.

After the approval by Congress and the people of Puerto Rico of the Puerto Rican Constitution, the United States advised the United Nations that it would no longer report with respect to Puerto Rico under article 73(e) of the United Nations Charter since Puerto Rico was now a self-governing territory.[28]

The characterization of the status of Puerto Rico was as follows:

Congress has agreed that Puerto Rico shall have under that constitution freedom from control or interference by the Congress in respect of internal government and administration subject only to compliance with applicable provisions of the Federal Constitution, the Puerto Rican Federal Relations Act, and the acts of Congress authorizing and approving the constitution as may be interpreted by judicial decision. Those laws which directed or authorized interference with matters of local government by the Federal Government have been repealed.[29]

---

[28] Memorandum by the Government of the United States of America concerning the cessation of transmission of information under art. 73(e) of the charter with regard to the Commonwealth of Puerto Rico. Annex II of U.N. Dec. A/AC. 35/L. 121, p. 8. "U.S. Mission to the United Nations," press release No. 1741, Aug. 28, 1953, p. 2.

[29] Memorandum by the Government of the United States of America concerning the cessation of transmission of information under art. 73(e) of the charter with regard to the Commonwealth of Puerto Rico. Annex II of U.N. Doc. A/AC. 35/L. 121, p. 8.

Mrs. Frances P. Bolton, Special Representative to the United Nations
General Assembly, was even more emphatic:

> The Federal Relations Act to which reference has been made has
> continued provisions of political and economic union which the people
> of Puerto Rico have wished to maintain. In this sense the relationships
> between Puerto Rico and the United States have not changed. It
> would be wrong, however, to hold that because this is so and has been
> so declared in Congress, the creation of the Commonwealth of Puerto
> Rico does not signify a fundamental change in the status of Puerto
> Rico. The previous status of Puerto Rico was that of a territory subject
> to the full authority of the Congress of the United States in all govern-
> mental matters. The previous constitution of Puerto Rico was in fact
> a law of the Congress of the United States, which we called an Organic
> Act. Congress only could amend the Organic Act of Puerto Rico. The
> present status of Puerto Rico is that of a people with a constitution of
> their own adoption, stemming from their own authority, which only
> they can alter or amend. The relationships previously established also
> by a law of the Congress, which only Congress could amend, have now
> become provisions of a compact of a bilateral nature whose terms may
> be changed only by common consent.[30]

The U.S. action was approved by the United Nations General Assembly.

In addition, in three cases the Congress has passed laws affecting Puerto
Rico and has made the enactment conditional upon express consent by the
Legislature of Puerto Rico.[31]

The opponents of compact argue primarily from the legislative history of
the statute itself. They first state there is a significant difference between
the phrase "in the nature of a compact" used in Public Law 600 and the
word "compact" used in Public Law 447 and the wording normally used
when a territory becomes a State which has been held to create a "compact":
"by ordinance irrevocable without the consent of the United States and the
people of said State." [32]

Not only, they say, did Congress not use the appropriate statutory language, but the legislative history confirms that no change in status was
intended. They cite primarily the committee reports which followed the
letter comment of the Secretary of Interior on the bill:

> The bill under consideration would not change Puerto Rico's funda-
> mental, political, social, and economic relationship to the United States.
> . . . This bill does not commit the Congress, either expressly or by
> implication, to the enactment of statehood legislation for Puerto Rico

---

[30] Statement by Hon. Frances P. Bolton, U.S. Representative, in the Fourth Committee, on the relationship between the United States and Puerto Rico, Nov. 3, 1953. P. 241,
"Report on the Eighth Session of the General Assembly of the United Nations," by Hon.
Frances P. Bolton and Hon. James P. Richards of the Committee on Foreign Affairs, pursuant to H. Res. 113, H. Rept. No. 1695 (83d Cong., 2d sess.).

[31] 72 Stat. 1375, 26 U.S.C.A. 5314 (tax on distilled spirits) ; 70 Stat. 572, 26 U.S.C.A.
4774 (tax on narcotic drugs and marihuana), but see *Valpais* v. *U.S.*, 289 F. 2d 607 (CA 1
1961) (act held applicable to Puerto Rico prior to consent) ; 75 Stat. 245 (joint resolution eliminating limitation on amount of Commonwealth bonded indebtedness). See also
Rept. No. 2174 (84th Cong., 2d sess., 1956). (Puerto Rico consent obtained prior to passage of continuation of processing tax on refined sugar.)

[32] E.g., Utah Enabling Act, act of July 16, 1894, 28 Stat. 107 ; Minnesota Enabling Act,
act of Feb. 26, 1857, 11 Stat. 166.

in the future. Nor will it in any way preclude a future determination by the Congress of Puerto Rico's ultimate political status.[33]

In addition, they note the statements of Commonwealth representatives before the committee:

As already pointed out, H.R. 7674 would not change the status of the island of Puerto Rico relative to the United States. It would not commit the United States for or against any specific future form of political formula for the people of Puerto Rico. It would not alter the powers of sovereignty acquired by the United States over Puerto Rico under the terms of the Treaty of Paris.[34]

. . . Mr. Chairman, I would like to make two comments: One, there would always be the way open to anybody who found an amendment to the Constitution went beyond the framework laid down by Congress, the right to go to the courts; and, secondly, the authority of the Government of the United States, the Congress, to legislate in case of emergency would always be there.[35]

Opponents of compact also argue that subsequent executive action in the United Nations cannot create legislative intent. In any event, the issue, they say, whether a territory is self-governing or non-self-governing territory for the purposes of article 73 (e) of the United Nations Charter is not relevant to the issue of compact.

Further, although there have been three cases where Congress adopted laws requiring the consent of Puerto Rico, there have been many more cases where Congress has passed laws and the executive branch has taken action substantially affecting Puerto Rico without Puerto Rican consent.[36]

The terms of any compact have been much debated.[37] In 1959, Commonwealth spokesmen testifying on the Fernos-Murray bill seemed to suggest that the compact embraced all laws covered by the Puerto Rico Federal Relations Act. They suggested that the tax exemption and the free access to the mainland market referred to in the Puerto Rican Federal Relations Act could not be changed without Puerto Rican consent.[38]

It has been suggested that the compact is narrower in scope: that what was intended was an affirmation that Congress would not declare Puerto

---

[33] H. Rept. No. 2275, 81st Cong., 2d sess., p. 3 ; see also S. Rept. No. 1779, 81st Cong., 2d sess., p. 3.

[34] Statement of Dr. Fernós Isérn, "Hearings Before the Committee on Public Lands," House of Representatives, 81st Cong., on H.R. 7674 and S. 3336, p. 63.

[35] Id. at p. 33. In addition, ibid., statement of Governor Muñoz Marín. See also the opinion of Irwin Silverman, Chief Counsel of the Office of Territories, rendered to Senator Malone, U.S. Senate, "Hearings Before the Committee on Interior and Insular Affairs," on S.J. Res. 151, pp. 40–45 (82d Cong., 2d sess.). Congressman Meader introduced a specific amendment on this point which was rejected, although the grounds for its defeat are unclear. 98 Cong. Rec. 6203, 7848.

[36] E.g., in the two tax statutes cited above, other sections of the same statute did not request Puerto Rican consent. Presumably Congress intended them to become valid with respect to Puerto Rico when passed. See also amendment by Congress of sec. 9 of Puerto Rican Federal Relations Act (Philippine Trade Agreement Revision Act of 1955, 69 Stat. 427) and changes in estate and gift tax provisions re Puerto Rican residents (72 Stat. 1674, 26 U.S.C.A. 2208, 2501).

[37] Statement of David M. Helfeld, Dean of the University of Puerto Rico School of Law, U.S. House of Representatives, "Hearings Before the Committee on Interior and Insular Affairs on H.R. 5945," p. 304 (88th Cong., 1st sess.).

[38] E.g., testimony of Gov. Muñoz Marín, U.S. Senate, "Hearings Before the Committee on Interior and Insular Affairs on S. 2023," pp. 50–53 (86th Cong., 1st sess.).

ulated prior to the grant of U.S. citizenship to Puerto Rico.[53] the grant in 1917 of Federal citizenship to Puerto Rico [54] did t the doctrine's applicability to Puerto Rico,[55] the expansion of s of Federal citizens in recent years suggests that the judiciary ely as heavily as before on the doctrine in determining the constitu- hts of U.S. citizens living in Puerto Rico. Recent constitutional ents give rise to the possibility that the fact of U.S. citizenship entral to the question of the nature of the future relationship he mainland and the island. Expansion of the spectrum of rights by the due process clauses of the 5th and 14th amendments to al Constitution to include areas previously believed protected only constitutions suggests that certain rights inhere in U.S. citizens of their place of residence.[56] Thus, U.S. citizenship carries with ersonal and institutional protections which cannot be encroached he Legislature of Puerto Rico or the Congress of the United States.

icability of Federal Laws

k of clarity concerning the applicability of Federal laws to Puerto s from (a) the interpretation of the effect of the 1950–52 legisla- section 9 of the Puerto Rico Federal Relations Act that provides laws of the United States *not locally inapplicable . . .* shall have force and effect in Puerto Rico as in the United States . . ."; [57] n many cases the obscure language of the particular Federal statute The question of the effect of the 1950–52 legislation on the lity of Federal law has been considered in a number of cases [58]

---

s born in Puerto Rico may have been, from the time of Puerto Rico's acquisition ted States, natural born U.S. citizens under the Constitution regardless of al action. *United States* v. *Wong Kim Ark* 169 U.S. 649 (1898). See *Gonzalez* 192 U.S. 1 (1904).

nstitutional rights of Federal citizenship appear to be the following: the right eely throughout the United States, the right to demand Federal protection and e and property, the right to peaceably assemble and petition for redress of the privilege of the writ of habeas corpus, right to use navigable waters, rights irtue of treaties with foreign powers (*Slaughter-House Cases* 83 U.S. (16 Wall.) (1872)), the right to access to the offices of the Federal Government and the rts (*Crandall* v. *State of Nevada* 73 U.S. (6 Wall.) 35, 43–44 (1867)). See ncurring opinion of Justice Douglas in *Bell* v. *Maryland* 378 U.S. 226, 250 pressing the view that the privileges and immunities of Federal citizenship ncreased; specifically, to include the right to be afforded public accommodations crimination.

v. *Porto Rico* 258 U.S. 298 (1922); *Fournier* v. *Gonzalez* 269 F. 2d 26 (C.A. 1,

., *Baker* v. *Carr*, 369 U.S. 186 (1962); *Kinsella* v. *Singleton*, 361 U.S. 234 lling v. *Sharpe*, 347 U.S. 497 (1954); cf. *Morgan* v. *Katzenbach*, 384 U.S. 641 S. v. *Monroe County*, 248 F. Supp. 316 (W.D.N.Y. 1965).

C.A. 734. (Italics supplied.)

sity jurisdiction) *Detres* v. *Lions Bldg. Corp.*, 234 F. 2d 596 (C.A. 7 1956) Supp. 699 (N.D. Ill. 1955); *López* v. *Resort Airlines* 18 F.R.D. 37 (S.D.N.Y. re *Lummus & Commonwealth Oil Refining Co., Inc.* 195 F. Supp. 47 (S.D.N.Y. ified by statutory amendment. 70 Stat. 658 (July 26, 1956); (Federal Fire- U.S. v. *Rios*, 140 F. Supp. 376 (D.P.R. 1956); (Three-judge court) *Mora* v. F. Supp. 610 (D.P.R. 1953); (Smith Act) *Carrión* v. *González*, 125 F. Supp. 819

Rico a "State" or "independent" without Puerto Rico's consent. It has also been suggested that the compact was intended to cover only those matters covered by the Puerto Rican constitution which was approved by the United States, treating Public Law 600 primarily as a home rule bill.

Opponents of compact seize upon this lack of clarity as additional evidence that no compact exists. They say if the terms of the compact are so much disputed, how can it be contended that Congress was clear and intended a compact?

In addition, questions have been raised concerning the theoretical limitations of a compact.[39] Opponents ask how far can this concept be extended before there is no longer a union? They ask, further, must not these limitations be clear before Congress can be said to have entered into such an agreement?

Of course, only the judiciary can definitively interpret existing legislation and as yet the courts have not ruled directly on the issue. A number of cases which have discussed this issue tangentially are noted in the footnote.[40]

The nature of the question and the nature of the judicial process is such, however, that the broad issue is unlikely to be raised, much less answered, for many, many years. The interpretation of a given law or the consequence of certain executive action in certain situations may give rise to a judicial decision which will assist in the resolution of the particular issue, but the larger questions will probably continue unresolved for some time.

Although only the Supreme Court can definitively decide the existing legal situation, some tentative conclusions may be put forward here.

There is no question that the 1950–52 legislation was intended to bring about a significant change in the previous relationship. The status represented by the prior Organic Acts was considered to be unsatisfactory by both Puerto Rico and the Federal Government. The 1950–52 legislation was directed toward accomplishing changes of fundamental importance which would give rise to a bilateral relationship and maximize participation by the people of Puerto Rico in the governmental processes which effect Puerto Rican life. Pursuant to this legislation Puerto Rico organized its own government with its powers arising from a constitution drafted by the people of Puerto Rico. This significant political change and the subsequent evolution of United States-Puerto Rico affairs substantially altered the factual background of United States-Puerto Rico relations. The factual change was of sufficient substance that it brought with it permanent legal consequences, although the record does not make clear their precise character.

The exact legal character and bounds of this bilateral relationship, the precise participation permissible under the existing arrangement as a matter of fact and law, varies depending on the circumstances and admits of no

---

[39] STACOM hearings, testimony of Abram Chayes, May 15, 1965.

[40] *Mora* v. *Torres*, 113 F. Supp. 309 (D.P.R. 1953); In the matter of Hilton Hotels, Inc., 37 L.R.R.M. 474 (P.R.L.R.B. 1955); *Figueroa* v. *Puerto Rico*, 232 F. 2d 615 (C.A. 11956); *R.C.A.* v. *Gobierno de la Capitol* (Sup. Ct. of Puerto Rico, Nov. 17, 1964); *U.S.* v. *County Board of Elections of Monroe County*, 248 F. Supp. 316 (W.D.N.Y. 1965); *Morgan* v. *Katzenbach*, 247 F. Supp. 196 (D.C.D.C. 1965) rev'd 384 U.S. 641 (1966). See also cases cited footnote 3, p. 59, infra.

sweeping generalization. Whether legislative or executive action is involved or whether the initiative rests in a particular case with the Federal or Puerto Rican Government will affect the matter considerably. In sum, the precise allocation of powers between the Puerto Rican Government and the Federal Government is a matter subject to determination only on the basis of the individual analysis of each area of governmental activity.

The bilateral character of the arrangement is most clear where the basic governmental structure of the Commonwealth is concerned. Here the procedure adopted indicates an intention not to change this without the consent of the Puerto Rican people. There may also be other areas involving the essential components of the association which are intended to be so covered. This should not be understood to mean that all Federal legislation and power over Puerto Rico was frozen in the exact molds in which that legislation was cast when the Commonwealth was established in 1952, and that such Federal legislation may not be changed in any respect without formal Puerto Rican consent. On the contrary, there are in effect two spheres of power: the congressional power and the power of the Government of Puerto Rico which arises from the fact that the government was created by the people of Puerto Rico. Within each sphere there are areas in which each government is free to act without consultation of the other government and without impinging on the principle against unilateral amendment where the fundamental governmental character of commonwealth is concerned.

Another consideration is the fact of U.S. citizenship which imposes upon both the Congress and the Legislature of Puerto Rico the obligation to protect the rights of citizens to participate effectively in the making of basic decisions which affect the nature of governmental forms. Therefore, neither Congress nor the Legislature of Puerto Rico may render ineffective the right of the Puerto Rican people to participate effectively in a decision about basic political forms which will affect their future.

The Congress should be responsive as it has in the past when the people of Puerto Rico in the future indicate the desirability of a change in the basic arrangement which has been concluded. Until that time, the Federal Government should act so as to maximize the participation by Puerto Rico in cases where the island will be affected by Federal Government action. This is consistent with the intent of the 1950–52 legislation and is in the best interests of both the Federal and Puerto Rican Governments.

2. Applicable Constitutional Provisions

The present legal relationship of Puerto Rico to the United States is the result of the applicability of various constitutional provisions and Federal laws to Puerto Rico.

The question of what U.S. constitutional provisions apply to Puerto Rico is unclear.[41] This lack of clarity results historically from the doctrine of

[41] It should be noted at this point that compact advocates argue that Puerto Rico no longer is governed by the territorial clause, and, therefore, it is no longer an unincorporated territory. "Puerto Rico, as declared by the United States before the United Nations in

"unincorporated" and "incorporated" territo Cases.[42] This doctrine holds that there is a which are incorporated and those that are not with it significant legal consequences. To Constituion applies fully; to an unincorporat mental provisions of the Constitution app tions . . . in favor of the liberty and property o absolute denial of authority . . . to do particular

Quite naturally a number of cases arose su given provision of the Constitution was so func unincorporated territory such as Puerto Rico.

The fifth-amendment requirement of indic sixth-amendment requirement of trial by jur not to apply to Puerto Rico.[44] In addition article I, section 8 has been held not applicable tions upon a State of the Union with respect and foreign commerce (art. I, sec. 8, clause levying of duties or imposts on imports (art. I not to apply to Puerto Rico prior to Public L only constitutional requirement specifically he Rico, although whether it is the 5th or 14th a

The sixth-amendment right to confrontati amendment right to trial by jury in common fifth-amendment right against double jeopar protection against bills of attainder or ex post to unincorporated territories.[48] The fourth-a unreasonable search and seizure,[49] the right in article 1, section 9, clause 2 [50] and the fifth-a pensation [51] quite likely do apply to unincorp

The continued applicability of the doctrine corporated territories to Puerto Rico is quest and the continuing vitality of the distinction Supreme Court in recent cases.[52] It should al

1953 and reaffirmed in 1959, has also stepped up from b territory) to the dignity of being an associated State June 3, 1959. The precise United States constitutio compact are unclear.

[42] *De Lima* v. *Bidwell* 182 U.S. 1 (1901); *Downes Dooley* v. *U.S.* 182 U.S. 222 (1901); *Armstrong* v. *U.S*

[43] *Downes* v. *Bidwell, supra,* at p. 294.

[44] *Porto Rico* v. *Tapia* 245 U.S. 639 (1918); *Balzac* v.

[45] *Downes* v. *Bidwell* 182 U.S. 244 (1901).

[46] *Buscaglia* v. *Ballester* 162 F. 2d 805 (C.A. 1 1947

[47] *Mora* v. *Mejias* 206 F. 2d 377 (C.A. 1 1953); *Col* 393 (C.A. 1 1958).

[48] *Dowdell* v. *U.S.* 221 U.S. 325 (1911); *Puerto Rico* 302 U.S. 253 (1937); *Grafton* v. *U.S.* 206 U.S. 333 (1 (1904); *Downes* v. *Bidwell* 182 U.S. 244, 277 (1901).

[49] *Best* v. *United States* 184 F. 2d 131, 138 (C.A. 1 1950

[50] *Eisentrager* v. *Forrestal* 174 F. 2d 961, 965 (C.A.D.C

[51] *Mitchell* v. *Harmony* 54 U.S. (13 How.) 115, 133 (457, 464 (U.S. Ct. of Cl. 1953).

[52] *Reid* v. *Covert* 354 U.S. 1, 14 (1957).

was for Althoug not affe the righ will not tional ri developr may be between covered the Fede by State regardle it basic upon by

3. App

The l Rico ari tion; (b "statuto the sam and (c) involved applicab

[53] Perso by the U congressio v. *William*

[54] The to travel care of l grievance gained by 36, 79–80 Federal c also the (1964), should be without d

[55] *Balza* 1959).

[56] See, (1960); (1966); (

[57] 48 U.

[58] (Dive rev'g. 136 1955); *I* 1961); cl arms Act *Mejias*, 1

without a clear rule emerging. The effect of the "not locally inapplicable" language in a particular case is also frequently unclear.[59]

The result is a series of congressional and administrative actions in connection with Puerto Rico without any consistent approach and in some cases without any apparent relationship to local needs. In many cases, Puerto Rico is treated in the same fashion as a State of the Union; in other cases, Puerto Rico is treated differently from the States. For example, U.S. income laws make a special exception for those individuals and corporations who are residents in Puerto Rico and receive income from Puerto Rican sources. If certain conditions are fulfilled, this Puerto Rican source income is not taxed at all of these residents.[60] Similarly, Puerto Rico is treated specially for the purposes of the Fair Labor Standards Act [61] and is specifically exempted from the jurisdiction of the Interstate Commerce Commission.[62] Similarly, under the various Federal poverty and grant-in-aid programs, Puerto Rico is treated in some cases like a State, in other cases quite uniquely: sometimes to its benefit; in others, to its detriment.[63] Again the U.S. district court in San Juan has slightly different jurisdiction than other Federal district courts,[64] and the Federal district judges in Puerto Rico are treated slightly less advantageously.[65] Some laws are sufficiently unclear so that they have resulted in litigation or have litigation pending.[66]

The above indicates the desirability from time to time of Puerto Rican and Federal officials being called together to discuss specific areas of uncertainty or concern so that the dialogue between the Puerto Rican and Federal Governments may be continued in a useful and meaningful way.

C. LEGAL ASPECTS OF PROSPECTIVE CHANGE

It should be noted that the following discussion is limited to legal issues only. The likelihood of any arrangement either as a transition measure or

---

(D.P.R. 1954) ; *U.S.* v. *Carrión,* 140 F. Supp. 226 (D.P.R. 1956) ; (General conspiracy statute) *Arbona* v. *Kenton,* 126 F. Supp. 366 (S.D.N.Y. 1954) ; (The Taft-Hartley Act) *Gosentino* v. *International Longshoremen's Association,* 126 F. Supp. 420 (D.P.R. 1954) ; *U.S.* v. *Mejias,* 131 F. Supp. 957 (D.P.R. 1955) ; but see *Hilton Hotels International, Inc. d/b/a Caribe Hilton Hotel and Local 24,918, Unión de Trabajadores de la Industria Gastronómica y Ramas Anexas de P.R.* 37 L.R.R.M 1474 (P.R.L.R.B. 1955) ; (The Fair Labor Standards Act) *Mitchell* v. *Rubio* 139 F. Supp. 379 (D.P.R. 1956) ; (Narcotics Drugs Import and Export Act and the Marihuana Tax Act) *Moreno Rió́s* v. *U.S.,* 256 F. 2d 68 (C.A. 1 1958) ; *Sanchez* v. *U.S.,* 256 F. 2d 73 (C.A. 1 1958).

[59] *Granville-Smith* v. *Granville-Smith,* 349 U.S. 1, 17 (1955).

[60] Domestic corporations doing business in Puerto Rico may also receive these benefits. The key sections of the Internal Revenue Code are sections 931 and 933. The subject is treated comprehensively in Mihaly, *Tax Advantages of Doing Business in Puerto Rico* 16 Stan. L. Rev. 75 (1963) and Novak, *A New Appraisal of Puerto Rico in Light of Recent Tax Legislation* 19 Tax L. Rev. 209 (1964).

[61] 29 U.S.C.A. 201–209.

[62] 48 U.S.C.A. 751.

[63] 78 Stat. 508 (poverty program) ; 79 Stat. 27 (Eelementary and Secondary Education Act of 1965) ; 42 U.S.C.A. 303(a) (old age assistance) : 42 U.S.C.A. 291(b) (hospital construction assistance).

[64] 48 U.S.C.A. 863.

[65] 28 U.S.C.A. 134 ; 28 U.S.C.A. 373 ; cf. 28 U.S.C.A. 371.

[66] E.g., *Securities and Exchange Commission* v. *Wong et al.* (D.P.R. Apr. 6, 1966).

under an improved or different status involves a high degree of political speculation and is outside the scope of this discussion.

1. Commonwealth

Proposals to improve and develop the Commonwealth would not appear to give rise to serious legal or constitutional problems. It is believed that, consistent with due process, the Federal Government and the Commonwealth may make such adjustments in the existing laws and regulations governing their relationships as are deemed appropriate.

2. Statehood

Prior to the accomplishment of Statehood, the present flexibility that Puerto Rico enjoys may legally be continued. Thus, transition measures which are contemplated may be enacted, limited only by due process considerations. The present exception to the Fair Labor Standards Act, the tax exemption, free access to the mainland market, and an external tariff different from the mainland United States could be available during any transition period prior to Statehood.

After Statehood, Puerto Rico's external tariff would have to be the same as the other States in the Union.[67] Continued tax exemption under Statehood would raise serious constitutional questions,[68] even though the word "taxes" is not repeated in the second, or uniformity, clause of article 1, section 8, clause 1 of the U.S. Constitution. On the other hand, special grant-in-aid and welfare legislation, including the Fair Labor Standards exception, could legally be made available after Statehood if the Congress made the appropriate finding that this aid is necessary to the economic welfare of Puerto Rico.

3. Independence

Proposals to lead Puerto Rico toward independence would appear to have no serious legal or constitutional objection. It is believed that, consistent with due process, the Federal Government and Puerto Rico may make such adjustments in the existing laws and regulations governing their relationship as is deemed appropriate.

After independence, the Federal Government may legally enter into arrangements with Puerto Rico to permit tax benefits and free access to the mainland market. This would, of course, have to be done by treaty. In addition, Puerto Rico under independence would be eligible for foreign aid funds available from the United States, other nations, and international agencies.

---

[67] U.S. Constitution, art 1, sec. 8, clause 1, and art. 1, sec. 9, clause 6.

[68] 2 *Willoughby on the Constitution of the United States* 683–694 (1929 2d ed.). The origin of the uniformity clause is discussed extensively in *Knowlton* v. *Moore*, 178 U.S. 41, 84–110 (1900). Congressional taxing power under art. 1, sec. 8, art. 1, sec. 9, and the 16th amendment is discussed in *Pollock* v. *Farmers' Loan and Trust Company*, 157 U.S. 429 (1895); *Flint* v. *Stone Tracy Company*, 220 U.S. 107 (1910); *Billings* v. *United States* 232 U.S. 261 (1914); *Brushaber* v. *Union Pacific Railroad Company*, 240 U.S. 1 (1916). The relationships of the equal protection clause or its equivalent to these provisions are discussed in *LaBelle Iron Works* v. *United States*, 256 U.S. 377, 392 (1921); *Steward Machine Co.* v. *Davis*, 301 U.S. 548, 584 (1937).

The Commission's Conclusions
and Recommendations *

INTRODUCTION

This Commission grew out of an exchange of letters released on July 25, 1962, between the late President John F. Kennedy and the then Governor of Puerto Rico, Luis Muñoz Marín, commemorating the 10th anniversary of the Commonwealth. Both recognized that despite ten years of extraordinary economic and social achievement, there was room for further institutional growth within the United States-Commonwealth relationship. They agreed that it was the proper time to consult the people of Puerto Rico concerning further development of the Commonwealth relationship; and that also, "both as a matter of fairness to all concerned and of establishing an unequivocal record," the people of Puerto Rico should be afforded the opportunity to express a status preference among a more fully developed Commonwealth, Statehood, and Independence.

The proposed principles underlying a more fully developed Commonwealth along with definitions of Statehood and Independence were contained in Joint Resolution No. 1 passed by the legislative assembly on December 3, 1962. Subsequent efforts, however, to develop with the Congress a procedure for consulting the people of Puerto Rico encountered obstacles of deeply felt differences over political status among the people of Puerto Rico, as well as of conflicting views about the validity and the reality of the status alternatives. Therefore, instead of attempting to formulate a procedure for conducting a referendum, Congress invited the Legislative Assembly of Puerto Rico to establish this joint Commission to "study all factors . . . which may have a bearing on the present and future relationship between the United States and Puerto Rico."*

In accordance with its mandate the Commission has conducted a contemporary review of Puerto Rico's status. It adopted, at the outset, a program of studies designed to insure systematic analysis of the most significant aspects of the United States-Puerto Rico relationship.

The Commission also held hearings in San Juan, P.R., during which extensive testimony was taken on three broad categories of questions affecting status: legal-constitutional in May 1965; social-cultural in July

---

*Public Law 88–271, Feb. 20, 1964 ; 78 Stat. 17.

* Report of the United States-Puerto Rico Commission on the Status of Puerto Rico (Washington: Government Printing Office, 1966), pp. 3-18.

1965; and economic in November–December 1965. Notice of the hearings was widely publicized in Puerto Rico and all who wished to be heard were given an opportunity to testify. In all, the Commission heard 123 witnesses over a period of 14 days comprising about 2,000 pages of testimony. A wide variety of experts on questions relevant to the status problem were also consulted and comment was invited from all who wished to do so.

There were no clearcut guidelines on how the Commission should proceed with its work. As far as can be determined, this is the first occasion, except for the month-long effort of the President's Committee for the Alteration of the Organic Act in 1943, that a comprehensive review of the status question has been undertaken by a joint United States-Puerto Rican group aided by professional staff and expert consultants. It is probably also the first time that public hearings concerning the cultural aspects of status were conducted during which witnesses offered specific testimony on cultural, social, and historical dimensions of the present status or proposed alternatives.

This Commission is profoundly aware that there is more to the subject than came within reach of its efforts. When the destiny of a people is at issue there can be no "final" or "complete" studies. For the principal subject is in the realm of a people's deepest commitments to its own ideals and values, and it is not given to commissioners or to scholars to know or understand all that underlies those ideals and values. The Commission believes, however, that the extensive product of its work reflects the sincerity of its effort to understand and delineate a complicated and sensitive question.

In this product, which will be available to the public, is included the verbatim, bilingual transcript of all the hearings; the summary of the discussion of a special panel of legal experts which was conducted on the legal and constitutional issues; the transcript of a staff and liaison staff presentation followed by a Commission discussion on economic questions; a series of background reports by leading scholars on major questions bearing upon the status issue; a bibliography of materials covering the broad range of United States-Puerto Rican relations; and staff studies and memorandums on technical and other questions bearing on the problem. In much of this documentation novel ground was explored. For example, despite the fact that the status question has in varying degrees been an issue in United States-Puerto Rico relations for over 60 years, no history of the status question was published until this Commission arranged to do so. Indeed, all of the special studies contain material which has been published for the first time. It is gratifying to note that already the material has been requested for use in academic institutions both in Puerto Rico and in the United States.

The cooperation received from the people of Puerto Rico, the Government of the Commonwealth of Puerto Rico, and the numerous departments and agencies of the Government of the United States has been outstanding. Noteworthy, too, has been the cooperation of the principal political parties and of other groups in Puerto Rico concerned with the status question.*

---

*The Commission regrets that the Independence Party representative resigned prior to the drafting of this report. However, in accordance with its mandate, the Commission thoroughly analyzed the Independence alternative.

The mainland Commissioners wish in particular to express their special gratitude for the generous courtesy and hospitality they received from the people of Puerto Rico who never permitted the great stakes that this issue holds for them to diminish the graciousness of their welcome. The Puerto Rico Commissioners wish in turn to express their deep appreciation to the mainland Commissioners for their sincere interest as well as for the effort and the time they devoted to the work of the Commission.

By the specific direction of the Commission at its final meeting, the Chairman wishes to acknowledge, and to express the great appreciation of the Commission for the leadership, imagination, and devotion of its Executive Secretary, Ambassador Ben S. Stephansky. Without his unremitting daily effort, his unflagging enthusiasm, and his sense of wise administration, there would have been no report. He has served the cause of United States-Puerto Rico relations well.

The devotion and loyalty of the entire staff was no less marked. They have worked diligently and effectively to provide the necessary background material, to prepare for hearings, to analyze testimony, and to assemble the facts and figures on which this report is based. Without their help, it would have been impossible for the Commission to carry out the President's directive within the time limit that was set.

This report consists of two parts. This part of the report, part I, contains the Commission's conclusions and recommendations resulting from the study. Part II is in the form of appendixes prepared by the staff and utilized by the Commissioners in arriving at their conclusions and recommendations and is devoted, respectively, to the legal–constitutional, the economic, the social–cultural factors of the status question, the history and the work of the Commission, and a selected bibliography on United States-Puerto Rico relations.

CONCLUSIONS

Before presenting its conclusions and recommendations, the Commission wishes to record its satisfaction that the bonds which unite Puerto Rico and the United States have been reaffirmed in the course of the Commission's work.

Both Puerto Rico and the United States share a common commitment to individual freedom, to fundamental human rights, and to the traditions of democratic, representative government. Both are vitally interested in the economic growth and in the political development of the Caribbean area, within which Puerto Rico has provided a worthy example of progress and stability. Finally, both Puerto Rico and the United States have pledged their resources and their efforts to the success of the Alliance for Progress in its historic mission for hemispheric development.

These mutual interests of Puerto Rico and the United States are the product of a history of increased understanding out of which has grown a

creative association. The foundation for both the mutual interests as well
as the creative association has been the common U.S. citizenship. In 1952,
77 percent of the people of Puerto Rico voted for their two principal
political parties that advocated, although in different forms, a permanent
union between Puerto Rico and the United States based upon common
U.S. citizenship; and this percentage has since increased steadily with each
election, reaching 94 percent in 1964.

Throughout its deliberations the Commission has been particularly aware
of the intimacy of the relationship between the United States and Puerto
Rico and of the obligation which the association imposes for the consideration of the wishes of the people of Puerto Rico. In full appreciation
of the importance of the maintenance of a mutually satisfactory relationship
between Puerto Rico and the mainland, the Commission presents the
following conclusions from its study of the factors bearing on the present
and future relationship between the United States and Puerto Rico.

The Commission's major conclusion is that all three forms of political
status—the Commonwealth, Statehood, and Independence—are valid and
confer upon the people of Puerto Rico equal dignity with equality of status
and of national citizenship. Any choice among them is to be made by the
people of Puerto Rico, and the economic, social, cultural, and security
arrangements which would need to be made under each of the three status
alternatives will require the mutual agreement and full cooperation of the
Government of the United States. A first step toward any change in
political status must be taken by the Puerto Rican people acting through
constitutional processes.

From the examination of the legal and constitutional factors affecting the
status question, the Commission concludes:

1. The policy governing the relationship between the United States and
Puerto Rico is and should continue to be based on the principles of mutual
consent and self-determination.

2. In accordance with this policy and these principles, it is essential to
any change in political status that Congress fully understand the wishes of
the people of Puerto Rico in order that it can be properly guided in working
with the people of Puerto Rico to carry out their wishes.

3. The right of the U.S. citizens of Puerto Rico to participate effectively
in decisions affecting their present and future welfare is protected by the
Constitution of the United States and the Constitution of Puerto Rico.

4. All three status alternatives—the Commonwealth, Statehood, and
Independence—are within the power of the people of Puerto Rico and the
Congress to establish under the Constitution.

5. As a form of political status, each alternative confers equal dignity and
equality of status.

From the examination of the sociocultural factors affecting the status
question, the Commission concludes:

6. Each of the three status positions contains an ideological dimension:
Each involves a concept of the identity of the people of Puerto Rico, an
interpretation of history, a way of life, and an aspiration for the future.

7. Each of the status alternatives is committed to the growth of Puerto

Rico's culture and the preservation of the Spanish language. Each alternative would require a different form of adjustment to fulfill its commitment.

8. Insofar as the questions of ideology and of culture and language are involved in arriving at a consensus regarding their future political status, it is the people of Puerto Rico themselves who must resolve these questions.

From the examination of the economic factors affecting the status question, the Commission concludes:

9. An examination of the economy of Puerto Rico with reference to political status involves the problem of comparing a pattern of growth under an existing set of institutional relationships which has resulted in impressive economic development, with patterns of economic growth under alternative institutional arrangements proposed by the advocates of statehood and independence.

10. Despite the substantial rates of economic growth of the past two decades, the continued economic growth and development of Puerto Rico is imperative. Puerto Rico's average per capita income is still 40 percent below that of the lowest income State of the Union. Furthermore, only through continued, rapid growth will it be possible to resolve such problems as the persistent high rate of unemployment, the uneven development of the island, inadequate transportation and communications, and the continuing need for further development of education and other basic public services.

11. An immediate or abrupt change in political status would involve serious economic risks and dislocations. These could be offset by special economic and financial arrangements which, in the case of Statehood, would clearly involve financial assistance well beyond the levels Puerto Rico is today receiving. In the case of Independence the costs of an abrupt change could be much greater. To allow for the adjustments required by a change to either Statehood or Independence, a carefully designed plan of transition would be necessary.

12. As far as economic standards alone are concerned, estimates regarding the time intervals required for transitions depend upon projections utilizing such criteria as growth rates of per capita income, comparative wage rates with the mainland, rate of unemployment, levels of investment in the public and private sectors, and growth rates under each of the status alternatives. For Independence there are such additional criteria as alternative sources for financing capital investment and the development of new export markets.

Professional economists differ as to when these projected criteria may be fulfilled. Professional estimates begin at a minimum of 15 years to a much longer period for Statehood; and even longer for Independence* unless there is more rapid economic development and integration of this hemisphere than can now be reasonably expected. However, the speed of

---

*The economist representing the Independence Party estimated at an economic presentation on Feb. 8–9, 1966, that the necessary economic adjustments might be effected within a period of 10 years after the granting of independence, but also estimated that a period of as long as 20 years might be required to insure an adequate margin of safety.

Puerto Rico's economic growth is such that any current estimates might be bettered by actual experience.

13. As Puerto Rico continues to develop, a time will come when the economic structure can more readily absorb the impact of a change to Statehood or Independence. It is therefore in the interest of proponents of such change to maximize Puerto Rico's economic growth, for as further growth is achieved the people of Puerto Rico will be able to weigh more realistically the economic costs and advantages of each of the status alternatives.

From the examination of all the foregoing factors affecting the status question, the Commission further concludes:

14. An expression of the will of the citizens of Puerto Rico by popular vote on the question of whether they wish to continue Commonwealth status capable of growth and development, or to change to either statehood or independence would be helpful to all concerned. The Commission recognizes, however, that it is for the people of Puerto Rico to decide whether, when, and in what manner they wish to express their preference. Such an expression should precede any change in status.

In this regard, the Commission wishes to note Puerto Rico Law No. 95, passed June 21, 1960, which permits the people of Puerto Rico to express a status preference. This law provides that 10 percent of the qualified electorate can bring about a plebiscite on the status issues without further legislation or executive action. Under this or any other law of similar intent that the Legislature of Puerto Rico is empowered to enact, the wishes of the people of Puerto Rico may be expressed.

RECOMMENDATIONS

Method for Constituting Ad Hoc Advisory Groups

The above conclusions and the facts underlying them point to the need, in the immediate future, for a method that provides for the consideration of proposals for improvement or growth of Commonwealth, or for change to Statehood or Independence.

The Commission recommends that procedures be devised which will permit the establishment of ad hoc joint advisory groups upon the initiative of the President of the United States and the Governor of Puerto Rico, acting jointly.

These ad hoc joint advisory groups would be composed of persons of the highest prestige and ability, and would consider problems affecting the relations between the Island and the Mainland referred to them by the President of the United States and the Governor of Puerto Rico. Each joint advisory group would report its conclusions and recommendations to the President and Congress of the United States and to the Governor and Legislative Assembly of Puerto Rico. The membership of each advisory group would be determined by the nature of the particular problem under consideration.

If the people of Puerto Rico should by plebiscite indicate their desire for Statehood or Independence, a joint advisory group or groups would be constituted to consider appropriate transition measures. If the people of Puerto Rico should maintain their desire for the further growth of the Commonwealth along the lines of the Commonwealth Legislative Assembly's Resolution No. 1 of December 3, 1962, or through other measures that may be conducive to Commonwealth growth, a joint advisory group or groups would be convened to consider these proposals.

DISCUSSION OF STATUS ALTERNATIVES

Contemporary Setting of the Status Question

The three status alternatives that stand today before the people of Puerto Rico are familiar concepts in the annals of Puerto Rico's history. They have some of their antecedents in the home rule, assimilist, and separatist political movements of the 19th century under Spain that led to Puerto Rico's Charter of Autonomy in 1897. They find their precedents in the status positions of the earliest political parties organized in Puerto Rico under United States rule, the Republican, the Federal, and the Union Parties. Indeed, in 1904 the Union Party in strikingly modern terms urged either statehood, independence, or self-rule under the American flag as the future status choices for Puerto Rico, and as early as 1922 it declared "that the creation of the Free Associated State of Puerto Rico . . . is the program of the party." Although the Free Associated State, as then described, differed materially from the Commonwealth as established in 1952, from that time to the present the three concepts have been regarded as the classic status agenda of the people of Puerto Rico.

Until the early 1940's, the status options were debated against the background of Puerto Rico's underdevelopment. The dignity that each status position aspired to confer upon Puerto Rico foundered on the stark fact that none of the status choices offered a way out of the island's persistent underdevelopment. Nor did a series of studies and inquiries, official and unofficial, produce any effective solutions for the dilemmas of underdevelopment. In Puerto Rico the status debate became a divisive and, at times, explosive agitation. In the United States the impression emerged that Puerto Rico was "not ready" for any of the three status alternatives, and the island was limited to minimal self-government, unilaterally bestowed by the United States under the Organic Acts of 1900 and 1917. The extension of U.S. citizenship to the people of Puerto Rico in 1917 did not change the political status of the island at that time but held prospects for the future.

The era of growth and development which began in the 1940's, and which has been accelerated after the postwar period during the past two decades, has established a totally new setting for the status question. The extraordinary transformation of a small, overpopulated island with severely limited natural resources in a brief span of time has been without parallel

or precedent.   The uniqueness of this achievement, which still eludes so
much of the underdeveloped world, can be noted in the most recent "Report
on the World Social Situation" of the United Nations Economic and Social Council, which states:

> "The performance of the developing countries as a whole would appear to
> have declined in the early 1960's . . . . It is an inescapable fact that, in spite
> of the national and international efforts the rate of progress in the low-income
> countries in recent years has been a disappointment."*

During these same "recent years" Puerto Rico has been among the four
most rapidly growing communities in the world.

Puerto Rico's growth has placed it in the class of the world's advancing
communities.   But its growth and development have not been in the economic
sphere alone.   While developing communities almost universally seem
doomed to wrestle with the discouraging problem of the degree of freedom
to be sacrificed in order to attain or accelerate economic growth, Puerto
Rico has been among the few where economic development has been accompanied by an ever-increasing participation of the people in its political
life.   Nor, as in so many communities struggling to grow, has a broadened
popular participation in political life been achieved through violence and
political instability.   In Puerto Rico a peaceful revolution has produced
a more stable democracy, an achievement that stands in sober contrast to
almost all of Latin America where only four countries have been able to
hold regular elections since 1948 in contrast to Puerto Rico's record of regular elections during the entire century.

There has been a visible growth of significant proportions in the skills of
public administration and administrative organization.   The social advances in health and education, in technical skills, in professionalization, and
in communications have been among the highest in the world.   A substantial investment in human development has brought recognition to Puerto
Rico as a place in which the purpose of development is the welfare of its
people.   New cultural expressions are developing with roots in Puerto Rico's
Hispanic-American history and tradition; presently flowering, in ever-increasing contact with other cultures, they are the product of growth in
literacy, advance in education, and of the extension of the opportunities for
a better life.   The American democratic form of government, including
the institutional structure of that government, and the legislative assistance
of the Congress have contributed substantially, in the opinion of this
Commission, to these achievements.

The sustained growth and development of Puerto Rico since the 1940's
has been a decisive factor in the progress of status evolution.   In 1943
President Franklin D. Roosevelt convened a President's Committee for the
Alteration of the Organic Act.   It was the first joint body of United States
and Puerto Rican representatives to consider fundamental problems of the
mainland-island relationship.   While many of the Committee's recommendations were not accepted, its conclusions were influential in the precedent-
breaking appointment of the first Puerto Rican governor in 1946.   In the

---

*"Report on the World Social Situation," Feb. 28, 1966, pp. 1–2.

next year the Elective Governor Act was adopted, again breaking new ground by providing for Puerto Rico to elect its own Governor with control over most of the island's executive appointments. Then, from 1950 to 1952, through a series of reciprocal acts by the United States and the people of Puerto Rico, the first Constitution of Puerto Rico was drafted by a Puerto Rican Constitutional Assembly and was adopted by popular referendum. The Constitution was approved by the President and the Congress and there was established the Commonwealth relationship.

These steps in the evolution of Puerto Rico's status constituted a complete reversal of the pessimistic assessment of the prewar years. From the view that Puerto Rico was too underdeveloped for any advance in political status, the rapid growth since World War II demonstrated beyond any doubt that Puerto Rico has full capacity to assume the responsibilities of self-government under any political status. The U.S. Congress recognized this capability when it participated with the people of Puerto Rico in the determination of Puerto Rico's political status in 1952; and it is in this tradition that the next steps in the evolution of the relationship between Puerto Rico and the United States have been explored as a matter of mutual interest, and with mutual esteem, by this bilateral Commission.

There is reason to be proud of the creation of a relationship between a small community and a large metropolitan democratic state which has fostered self-government and self-determination while achieving a truly phenomenal economic and social development. Those who have studied Puerteo Rico's progress, while acknowledging the great importance of U.S. economic aid to Puerto Rico and the flexible treatment reserved for Puerto Rico within the American constitutional framework, have properly given primary recognition to the genius and the energy of the people of Puerto Rico released by a generation of unusual men from the Island and the Mainland who discovered and learned to utilize the range of democratic and creative experimentation inherent in the fabric of Puerto Rico's relationship with the United States. A debt of gratitude is owed this generation, because the future political status of Puerto Rico—whether it will be continued and developed Commonwealth, Statehood, or Independence—will have evolved from the present threshold of Puerto Rico's achievements.

Commonwealth

The Commonwealth status which the people of Puerto Rico and the people of the continental United States agreed upon through a series of acts between 1950 and 1952 is a unique relationship. A thread of creativity has characterized the relationship between Puerto Rico and the United States from the very beginning, arising from the confrontation of two cultures initially strange to each other and from the need for a kind of relationship that could encourage the growth of a crowded, underdeveloped island.

The Commonwealth relationship was novel in the method of its creation. It was established through bilateral agreement between the people of Puerto Rico and the Congress of the United States. The steps in the procedure were similar to the familiar ones of Enabling Act procedures for the admission of States to the Federal Union, but without the result of creating a federal state. There was created, instead, a new form of federal relationship. It was based upon two spheres of government—that of constitutional self-government within Puerto Rico, and that of the Federal Government—with the two spheres of government connected by the applicable parts of the Federal Constitution and by the Federal Relations Act.

There was a new departure, also, in the intention that the relationship could continue indefinitely or could be changed. It was clearly understood that the relationship was not to be interpreted as being a transition step toward any other status. There could be a new decision by the people of Puerto Rico and the Congress of the United States, but Commonwealth was regarded as a status valid in itself.

Although the commonwealth relationship has operated successfully for over 14 years, it has inevitably, as in the evolving Federal-State relationship, revealed some undefined legal, political, and economic boundaries. For this reason, as well as because of strong opposition from the proponents of statehood and independence, the Commonwealth has been the subject of continuous debate from the time it was inaugurated. The debate has often produced misunderstanding and confusion.

With respect to questions raised on the subject of the compact, the Supreme Court of the United States is, of course, the ultimate interpreter of the Constitution and it has not declared itself on these questions. The weight of legal scholarship sustains the innovative power of the Federal Government to create a new form of association—including a binding association—in accordance with the desires of the people of Puerto Rico. It is clear that the U.S. Government entered into a solemn agreement with the Puerto Rican people in 1952 and that the agreement, referred to in the legislation as the compact, bears permanent legal consequences. What the Supreme Court would find the precise legal consequences to be of the bilateral arrangement entered into in 1952 is a matter of conjecture. Nor is it possible to say what procedure, if any, the Court would require for either its clarification or modification. With regard to these and other questions, the Commission feels that there has been an excess of legalistic, somewhat academic, controversy.

The Commission does have views on the political character of the commonwealth relationship created in 1950–52. The relationship is politically and morally valid. It constitutes a solemn undertaking, based upon mutual consent, between the people of the United States acting through their Federal Government and the people of Puerto Rico acting directly as well as through their established governmental processes. It is absolutely clear that the people of both communities are pledged irrevocably to the rights of self-government and to the guarantees of fundamental human rights protected by both constitutions. A solemn undertaking of such profound character between the Federal Government and a community of U.S. citizens is incompatible with the concept of unilateral revocation. It is inconceivable that either the United States or Puerto Rico would, by an act of unilateral revocation, undermine the very foundation of their common progress: the fundamental political and economic relationships which were established on the basis of mutuality.

A great deal has been said during the status debate of the last dozen years about the permanency of the relationship. Since the underlying validity of the relationship is its bilateral character, it will be as permanent as the people of Puerto Rico and the people of the United States wish it to be. As noted earlier, however, any future change in political status by mutual consent is not foreclosed.

The key to the continuation and development of the relationship between Puerto Rico and the mainland is U.S. citizenship. This citizenship carries with it basic personal and institutional protections which cannot be encroached upon by the Legislature of Puerto Rico or the Congress of the United States. Present constitutional doctrine, therefore, would not permit any action rendering ineffective the right of U.S. citizens of Puerto Rico to participate in the determination of their future, whether it will be continued and developed Commonwealth, Statehood, or Independence.

One of the consequences of the prolonged status debate in Puerto Rico has been that in contrast to the great vitality continuously evident with regard to economic and social development, there has been only limited institutional evolution of the Commonwealth idea within the federal relationship.

It is appropriate that the people of Puerto Rico should seek a more perfect Commonwealth, unless they choose another status. This is all the more appropriate for two societies as vitally alive and as rapidly changing as those of Puerto Rico and the United States. Since the growth must primarily meet the needs of Puerto Rico, the initiative lies there. The Commission believes that any process of further development would best be accomplished proceeding step by step as the needs dictate. In this manner, the principles contained in Joint Resolution No. 1 of December 3, 1962, should now be pursued, as should also other pertinent proposals that may be conducive to Commonwealth growth.

The Commission recognizes the Commonwealth as a dignified, legal, and creative political status, which will be permanent if the people of Puerto Rico wish to retain it. The fact, however, that the Commonwealth status contains the capacity for economic growth may at the same time make another political status, either Statehood or Independence, more viable. One of the virtues of the Commonwealth is the fact that it possesses a flexibility which will permit future changes within itself and which also permits freedom of choice of any alternative status that may be the future mutual desire of Puerto Rico and the United States.

Statehood

Statehood has from the beginning of the relationship between Puerto Rico and the United States been one of the articulate status aspirations. Although not all U.S. citizens are residents of States, the grant of U.S. citizenship to the people of Puerto Rico in 1917 made statehood a natural goal of many people of Puerto Rico. The development of a sturdy tradition and experience of self-government in Puerto Rico, the emergence of an able political leadership, and the creation of a growing economy with an increasing base for future growth have made Statehood a realistic possibility.

It is the belief of the Commission that Puerto Rico is at a stage in its history where the question of status should be elevated above partisanship. No area has ever achieved Statehood without a broad public demand transcending party lines.

The road to Statehood within the American Federal Union is familiar. The first prerequisite is a stable political and economic community; the second is the sustained desire for Statehood actively expressed over a period of time by a clear majority of the community; and the third is the willingness of the American people acting through their constitutional forms to accept the community as a new State, which, once admitted into the Union, would have all the rights and also all the responsibilities of the existing States.

Puerto Rico is a stable political community fully capable, by virtue of its demonstrated capacity for democratic self-government, of assuming the responsibilities of Statehood.

Economics is one of the vital factors in a Puerto Rican decision to seek or a congressional decision to grant Statehood. It has also proved to be the most discussed. The extensive economic studies which have been conducted do not clearly resolve the question of whether Puerto Rico is now prepared, or if not now, when in the future Puerto Rico will be prepared to assume the economic responsibilities and adjustments of statehood. Unless an appropriate substitute for Puerto Rico's present special economic arrangements can be provided, it is clear that were Statehood to be granted now, it would have severe and probably disastrous consequences. Economic studies, however, indicate that sustained economic growth under the present status and a continuation of the special economic arrangements will make Statehood with adequate but not extraordinary or unprecedented provision for transition fully possible without severe risks. Professional estimates for this begin at a minimum of 15 years to a much longer period. When this is depends on several factors any one or any combination of which could be controlling: (*a*) the future rate and character of Puerto Rican economic growth; (*b*) how long the special economic arrangements will continue; (*c*) what transitional arrangements Congress would make at the time Statehood would be voted; (*d*) what economic advantages would flow from the psychological effects of Statehood; and (*e*) what possible economic risks the people of Puerto Rico might be willing to assume in order to attain Statehood.

Since on balance these factors are more political than economic, and since all of them wait upon future events, the Commission cannot predict the time when Statehood would be economically feasible. Should the people of Puerto Rico decide they want Statehood, the economic questions would have then to be faced jointly by the people of Puerto Rico and by the Congress as they exist at that time. Until that time, or until more economic evidence is available, it is not helpful to the people of Puerto Rico to claim that the economic question of Statehood is not potentially a very serious one. It is equally not helpful to the people of Puerto Rico to assert that economic analysis indicates that Statehood would be economically disastrous for as far into the future as economists can see. Neither extreme position is supported by the facts as they can presently be known and the people of Puerto Rico should make any judgment on this question with these considerations in mind.

The other and probably now most important requirement for Statehood is the achievement of a clear majority for Statehood. Although there are no hard and fast rules in the American experience, it is evident that Congress acts favorably on a Statehood bill only when convinced that such a clear majority of the citizens concerned seek Statehood as a goal in itself from a confident and informed desire to meet its rigorous responsibilities and enjoy its privileges. Such a positive climate of consensus and understanding is a sine qua non to the achievement of Statehood for Puerto Rico. It would also be persuasive in order for Congress to enact whatever transitional arrangements were necessary to offset whatever economic burdens, severe or mild, in practice developed. None of the many witnesses heard by the Commission was able to inform the Commission, with an acceptable degree of conviction, how many people in Puerto Rico favor or oppose statehood as the ultimate status of Puerto Rico.

There is a cultural question relating to Statehood. If Puerto Rico became a State it would be a case of an area possessing a homogeneous, distinctive culture being incorporated into the United States. The experience with Hawaii, although so very different in many important ways, attests to the capacity of the U.S. citizens and the union of States to develop full Statehood with cultural diversity and without territorial contiguity. Statehood would necessarily involve a cultural and language accommodation to the rest of the federated States of the Union. The Commission does not see this as an insurmountable barrier, nor does this require the surrender of the Spanish language nor the abandonment of a rich cultural heritage. Nevertheless, the Commission expects that a decision for Statehood would denote a desire of the Puerto Rican people to share as well as contribute to the cultural heritage of the American people, to be an integral part of the American Nation as well as a State in the Federal Union.

Since it is for Congress and not for this Commission to grant Statehood if and when it is appropriately requested, it remains only to reiterate that the indispensable next step in this process, if Statehood is to be Puerto Rico's destiny, is a Puerto Rican decision to seek Statehood. Whether, when, and in what way this decision to seek Statehood should be taken is a matter solely for the Puerto Rican people to decide just as the final response to such an initiative is up to Congress and the President.

Independence

Independence is a legitimate and dignified aspiration for the people of Puerto Rico and is available as a status alternative if the people of Puerto

Rico so choose. Declarations by Presidents representing the two main political parties of the United States during the past 25 years have consistently stated that whenever it is the clear, expressed will of the people of Puerto Rico to be independent, the procedures leading to Independence would be initiated in accordance with the principle of self-determination.

The principle of self-determination requires that Independence could be established only by democratic majority of the people of Puerto Rico. In the 1964 general elections the Independence Party polled only 2.7 percent of the popular vote.

As in the case of the other status alternatives, the growth and development of Puerto Rico during the past 25 years makes a path to Independence more discernible. Puerto Rico, politically, is fully capable of assuming the responsibilities of democratic self-government as an independent republic. In fact, Puerto Rico is already serving as a training center for developing countries in a broad range of governmental and private activities.

Projections regarding the period of time required, from an economic point of view, for transition to Independence are very difficult for the reason that there are significant unknowns and intangibles. To avoid serious disruption of the economy, a period of preparation of unknown duration before Independence was granted would be necessary for Puerto Rico to acquire such economic instruments as control over its monetary system and its balance of payments, while also developing some of the basic new institutions needed to guide a transition to Independence. If the preparatory period were successful, most of the transition could take place after Independence was granted.

The Commission recognizes that different economic criteria need to be applied in the case of Independence. Two important ones are (1) the ability of an independent republic to find substitute sources for financing capital formation, and (2) the ability to develop alternative export markets. The position of the Independence advocates is that the degree of transformation of the Puerto Rican economy necessary to satisfy these two criteria could be accomplished in the course of a 25-year transition period. Conceivably, if there were sufficient sacrifice, the criterion of financing capital formation could be satisfied in a transition period of this length of time. A much longer period would probably be necessary, however, before a sufficient degree of economic and institutional transformation could take place elsewhere in the Western Hemisphere for a Republic of Puerto Rico to have the export markets necessary to sustain economic growth.

For continued progress under Independence, Puerto Rico would need to seek a new set of relationships which could substitute or at least supplement its present vital relationship with the United States. The conditions of regional economic integration permitting the pattern of trade and industry Puerto Rico would require for its vitality do not yet fully exist in either the Caribbean or in Latin America. It is difficult at present, therefore, to foresee Puerto Rican Independence without sustained generous amounts of aid from the United States, other nations, and international agencies on a considerably larger scale than such aid is or has been granted to countries of the size of Puerto Rico.

Rico a "State" or "independent" without Puerto Rico's consent. It has also been suggested that the compact was intended to cover only those matters covered by the Puerto Rican constitution which was approved by the United States, treating Public Law 600 primarily as a home rule bill.

Opponents of compact seize upon this lack of clarity as additional evidence that no compact exists. They say if the terms of the compact are so much disputed, how can it be contended that Congress was clear and intended a compact?

In addition, questions have been raised concerning the theoretical limitations of a compact.[39] Opponents ask how far can this concept be extended before there is no longer a union? They ask, further, must not these limitations be clear before Congress can be said to have entered into such an agreement?

Of course, only the judiciary can definitively interpret existing legislation and as yet the courts have not ruled directly on the issue. A number of cases which have discussed this issue tangentially are noted in the footnote.[40]

The nature of the question and the nature of the judicial process is such, however, that the broad issue is unlikely to be raised, much less answered, for many, many years. The interpretation of a given law or the consequence of certain executive action in certain situations may give rise to a judicial decision which will assist in the resolution of the particular issue, but the larger questions will probably continue unresolved for some time.

Although only the Supreme Court can definitively decide the existing legal situation, some tentative conclusions may be put forward here.

There is no question that the 1950–52 legislation was intended to bring about a significant change in the previous relationship. The status represented by the prior Organic Acts was considered to be unsatisfactory by both Puerto Rico and the Federal Government. The 1950–52 legislation was directed toward accomplishing changes of fundamental importance which would give rise to a bilateral relationship and maximize participation by the people of Puerto Rico in the governmental processes which effect Puerto Rican life. Pursuant to this legislation Puerto Rico organized its own government with its powers arising from a constitution drafted by the people of Puerto Rico. This significant political change and the subsequent evolution of United States-Puerto Rico affairs substantially altered the factual background of United States-Puerto Rico relations. The factual change was of sufficient substance that it brought with it permanent legal consequences, although the record does not make clear their precise character.

The exact legal character and bounds of this bilateral relationship, the precise participation permissible under the existing arrangement as a matter of fact and law, varies depending on the circumstances and admits of no

---

[39] STACOM hearings, testimony of Abram Chayes, May 15, 1965.
[40] *Mora* v. *Torres*, 113 F. Supp. 309 (D.P.R. 1953) ; In the matter of Hilton Hotels, Inc., 37 L.R.R.M. 474 (P.R.L.R.B. 1955) ; *Figueroa* v. *Puerto Rico*, 232 F. 2d 615 (C.A. 11956) ; *R.C.A.* v. *Gobierno de la Capitol* (Sup. Ct. of Puerto Rico, Nov. 17, 1964) ; *U.S.* v. *County Board of Elections of Monroe County*, 248 F. Supp. 316 (W.D.N.Y. 1965) ; *Morgan* v. *Katzenbach*, 247 F. Supp. 196 (D.C.D.C. 1965) rev'd 384 U.S. 641 (1966). See also cases cited footnote 3, p. 59, infra.

sweeping generalization. Whether legislative or executive action is involved or whether the initiative rests in a particular case with the Federal or Puerto Rican Government will affect the matter considerably. In sum, the precise allocation of powers between the Puerto Rican Government and the Federal Government is a matter subject to determination only on the basis of the individual analysis of each area of governmental activity.

The bilateral character of the arrangement is most clear where the basic governmental structure of the Commonwealth is concerned. Here the procedure adopted indicates an intention not to change this without the consent of the Puerto Rican people. There may also be other areas involving the essential components of the association which are intended to be so covered. This should not be understood to mean that all Federal legislation and power over Puerto Rico was frozen in the exact molds in which that legislation was cast when the Commonwealth was established in 1952, and that such Federal legislation may not be changed in any respect without formal Puerto Rican consent. On the contrary, there are in effect two spheres of power: the congressional power and the power of the Government of Puerto Rico which arises from the fact that the government was created by the people of Puerto Rico. Within each sphere there are areas in which each government is free to act without consultation of the other government and without impinging on the principle against unilateral amendment where the fundamental governmental character of commonwealth is concerned.

Another consideration is the fact of U.S. citizenship which imposes upon both the Congress and the Legislature of Puerto Rico the obligation to protect the rights of citizens to participate effectively in the making of basic decisions which affect the nature of governmental forms. Therefore, neither Congress nor the Legislature of Puerto Rico may render ineffective the right of the Puerto Rican people to participate effectively in a decision about basic political forms which will affect their future.

The Congress should be responsive as it has in the past when the people of Puerto Rico in the future indicate the desirability of a change in the basic arrangement which has been concluded. Until that time, the Federal Government should act so as to maximize the participation by Puerto Rico in cases where the island will be affected by Federal Government action. This is consistent with the intent of the 1950–52 legislation and is in the best interests of both the Federal and Puerto Rican Governments.

2. Applicable Constitutional Provisions

The present legal relationship of Puerto Rico to the United States is the result of the applicability of various constitutional provisions and Federal laws to Puerto Rico.

The question of what U.S. constitutional provisions apply to Puerto Rico is unclear.[41] This lack of clarity results historically from the doctrine of

---

[41] It should be noted at this point that compact advocates argue that Puerto Rico no longer is governed by the territorial clause, and, therefore, it is no longer an unincorporated territory. "Puerto Rico, as declared by the United States before the United Nations in

"unincorporated" and "incorporated" territories set forth in the Insular Cases. [42] This doctrine holds that there is a difference between territories which are incorporated and those that are not and that this difference brings with it significant legal consequences. To incorporated territories the Constituion applies fully; to an unincorporated territory, only the fundamental provisions of the Constitution applied, "the general prohibitions . . . in favor of the liberty and property of the citizen . . . which are an absolute denial of authority . . . to do particular acts." [43]

Quite naturally a number of cases arose subsequently testing whether a given provision of the Constitution was so fundamental that it applied to an unincorporated territory such as Puerto Rico.

The fifth-amendment requirement of indictment by grand jury and the sixth-amendment requirement of trial by jury have specifically been held not to apply to Puerto Rico.[44] In addition the uniformity provision in article I, section 8 has been held not applicable.[45] The constitutional restrictions upon a State of the Union with respect to the regulation of interstate and foreign commerce (art. I, sec. 8, clause 3) and prohibition upon the levying of duties or imposts on imports (art. I, sec. 10, clause 2) were held not to apply to Puerto Rico prior to Public Law 600.[46] Due process is the only constitutional requirement specifically held to be applicable to Puerto Rico, although whether it is the 5th or 14th amendment is not clear.[47]

The sixth-amendment right to confrontation of witnesses, the seventh-amendment right to trial by jury in common law cases, and, probably, the fifth-amendment right against double jeopardy and the first-amendment protection against bills of attainder or ex post facto laws are not applicable to unincorporated territories.[48] The fourth-amendment protection against unreasonable search and seizure,[49] the right to the writ of habeas corpus in article 1, section 9, clause 2 [50] and the fifth-amendment right to just compensation [51] quite likely do apply to unincorporated territories.

The continued applicability of the doctrine of unincorporated versus incorporated territories to Puerto Rico is questioned by compact advocates and the continuing vitality of the distinction has been questioned by the Supreme Court in recent cases.[52] It should also be noted that the doctrine

---

1953 and reaffirmed in 1959, has also stepped up from being a territory (an unincorporated territory) to the dignity of being an associated State." Speech of Gov. Muñoz Marín, June 3, 1959. The precise United States constitutional provisions which apply under compact are unclear.

[42] *De Lima* v. *Bidwell* 182 U.S. 1 (1901) ; *Downes* v. *Bidwell* 182 U.S. 244 (1901) ; *Dooley* v. *U.S.* 182 U.S. 222 (1901) ; *Armstrong* v. *U.S.* 182 U.S. 243 (1901).

[43] *Downes* v. *Bidwell, supra,* at p. 294.

[44] *Porto Rico* v. *Tapia* 245 U.S. 639 (1918) ; *Balzac* v. *Porto Rico* 258 U.S. 298 (1922).

[45] *Downes* v. *Bidwell* 182 U.S. 244 (1901).

[46] *Buscaglia* v. *Ballester* 162 F. 2d 805 (C.A. 1 1947) ; cert. den. 332 U.S. 816 (1947).

[47] *Mora* v. *Mejias* 206 F. 2d 377 (C.A. 1 1953) ; *Colon-Rosich* v. *Puerto Rico* 256 F. 2d 393 (C.A. 1 1958).

[48] *Dowdell* v. *U.S.* 221 U.S. 325 (1911) ; *Puerto Rico* v. *Shell Co. (P.R.) Limited, et al* 302 U.S. 253 (1937) ; *Grafton* v. *U.S.* 206 U.S. 333 (1907) ; *Kepner* v. *U.S.* 195 U.S. 100 (1904) ; *Downes* v. *Bidwell* 182 U.S. 244, 277 (1901).

[49] *Best* v. *United States* 184 F. 2d 131, 138 (C.A. 1 1950).

[50] *Eisentrager* v. *Forrestal* 174 F. 2d 961, 965 (C.A.D.C. 1949).

[51] *Mitchell* v. *Harmony* 54 U.S. (13 How.) 115, 133 (1852) ; *Turney* v. *U.S.* 115 F. Supp. 457, 464 (U.S. Ct. of Cl. 1953).

[52] *Reid* v. *Covert* 354 U.S. 1, 14 (1957).

was formulated prior to the grant of U.S. citizenship to Puerto Rico.[53] Although the grant in 1917 of Federal citizenship to Puerto Rico [54] did not affect the doctrine's applicability to Puerto Rico,[55] the expansion of the rights of Federal citizens in recent years suggests that the judiciary will not rely as heavily as before on the doctrine in determining the constitutional rights of U.S. citizens living in Puerto Rico.   Recent constitutional developments give rise to the possibility that the fact of U.S. citizenship may be central to the question of the nature of the future relationship between the mainland and the island.   Expansion of the spectrum of rights covered by the due process clauses of the 5th and 14th amendments to the Federal Constitution to include areas previously believed protected only by State constitutions suggests that certain rights inhere in U.S. citizens regardless of their place of residence.[56]   Thus, U.S. citizenship carries with it basic personal and institutional protections which cannot be encroached upon by the Legislature of Puerto Rico or the Congress of the United States.

3. Applicability of Federal Laws

The lack of clarity concerning the applicability of Federal laws to Puerto Rico arises from (a) the interpretation of the effect of the 1950–52 legislation; (b) section 9 of the Puerto Rico Federal Relations Act that provides "statutory laws of the United States *not locally inapplicable* . . . shall have the same force and effect in Puerto Rico as in the United States . . .";[57] and (c) in many cases the obscure language of the particular Federal statute involved.   The question of the effect of the 1950–52 legislation on the applicability of Federal law has been considered in a number of cases [58]

---

[53] Persons born in Puerto Rico may have been, from the time of Puerto Rico's acquisition by the United States, natural born U.S. citizens under the Constitution regardless of congressional action.   *United States* v. *Wong Kim Ark* 169 U.S. 649 (1898).   See *Gonzalez* v. *Williams* 192 U.S. 1 (1904).

[54] The constitutional rights of Federal citizenship appear to be the following : the right to travel freely throughout the United States, the right to demand Federal protection and care of life and property, the right to peaceably assemble and petition for redress of grievances, the privilege of the writ of habeas corpus, right to use navigable waters, rights gained by virtue of treaties with foreign powers (*Slaughter-House Cases* 83 U.S. (16 Wall.) 36, 79–80 (1872)), the right to access to the offices of the Federal Government and the Federal courts (*Crandall* v. *State of Nevada* 73 U.S. (6 Wall.) 35, 43–44 (1867)).   See also the concurring opinion of Justice Douglas in *Bell* v. *Maryland* 378 U.S. 226, 250 (1964), expressing the view that the privileges and immunities of Federal citizenship should be increased ; specifically, to include the right to be afforded public accommodations without discrimination.

[55] *Balzac* v. *Porto Rico* 258 U.S. 298 (1922) ; *Fournier* v. *Gonzalez* 269 F. 2d 26 (C.A. 1, 1959).

[56] See, *e.g.*, *Baker* v. *Carr*, 369 U.S. 186 (1962) ; *Kinsella* v. *Singleton*, 361 U.S. 234 (1960) ; *Bolling* v. *Sharpe*, 347 U.S. 497 (1954) ; cf. *Morgan* v. *Katzenbach*, 384 U.S. 641 (1966) ; *U.S.* v. *Monroe County*, 248 F. Supp. 316 (W.D.N.Y. 1965).

[57] 48 U.S.C.A. 734.   (Italics supplied.)

[58] (Diversity jurisdiction) *Detres* v. *Lions Bldg. Corp.*, 234 F. 2d 596 (C.A. 7 1956) rev'g. 136 Supp. 699 (N.D. Ill. 1955) ; *López* v. *Resort Airlines* 18 F.R.D. 37 (S.D.N.Y. 1955) ; *In re Lummus & Commonwealth Oil Refining Co., Inc.* 195 F. Supp. 47 (S.D.N.Y. 1961) ; clarified by statutory amendment.   70 Stat. 658 (July 26, 1956) ; (Federal Firearms Act) *U.S.* v. *Rios*, 140 F. Supp. 376 (D.P.R. 1956) ; (Three-judge court) *Mora* v. *Mejias*, 115 F. Supp. 610 (D.P.R. 1953) ; (Smith Act) *Carrión* v. *González*, 125 F. Supp. 819

The Commission conceives the achievement of an independent status, if desired by the people of Puerto Rico, not as an abrupt separation but as a series of adjustments along the Philippine pattern, resulting in amicable relations. Conceived in this way Independence would inevitably retain many of the characteristics of an older friendship and mutual understanding. It should be noted that Independence would carry the burden of successfully negotiating a set of new treaties and other agreements with other countries, international agencies, private investors, and the United States.

Under independent status Puerto Rico would probably continue to develop its cosmopolitan life. While an independent status assumes the emergence of a national spirit strong enough to organize, sustain, and meet the challenges of an independent community, for Puerto Rico this does not necessarily imply a narrow and self-defeating nationalism.

DISCUSSION OF RECOMMENDATIONS

In formulating its recommendations to provide for joint advisory groups the Commission had in mind several factors which have come to light in the course of its study and deliberations. First, is the factor of the Commonwealth's continued success. As noted earlier, the growth under Commonwealth not only serves to validate its own position but is essential also to make possible the realization of any other status without prohibitive hardships.

The second factor is the division among the people of Puerto Rico with regard to the status choices. These divisions have both ideological and political roots. Status choices, the Commission has come to see, are in a sense political "subcultures" within Puerto Rico's society. Each status viewpoint holds an interpretation of history, a way of life, a concept of the Puerto Rican identity, and an aspiration for a Puerto Rican destiny. Ideological differences alone make consensus difficult, but that difficulty is nurtured by the partisan political character of the status parties and by electoral competition. Thus, political opposition and ideology regularly enforce one another to intensify the conflict over status. This has been evident to the Commission in the course of its work and for that matter has beeen evident to the people of Puerto Rico themselves during the past dozen years. The Commission believes that the recommended ad hoc advisory groups may be useful in channeling the status debate along more constructive lines.

A third factor which underlies the Commission's interest in a joint advisory mechanism is what might be termed the "problems of progress" now evident in Puerto Rico. Few communities in the world have undergone such profound and far-reaching changes in so short a time as has Puerto Rico. Puerto Rico is learning that modernization is difficult and that rapid modernization multiplies the difficulties. As old problems are resolved, new ones are created. Questions inevitably will be raised with respect to

the flexibilities and the special arrangements that characterize the relationship. Furthermore, as society and class structure are altered, new horizons
and new aspirations and new conflicts inevitably emerge.

It is for these reasons that the Commission has recommended that a
mechanism be established for the consideration, from time to time, of
improvements in the Commonwealth relationship, or of measures of transition to Statehood or Independence depending upon the choice expressed by
the people of Puerto Rico.

PUERTO RICO SINCE COLUMBUS

From Luis Muñoz Marín, Puerto Rico Since Columbus
(New York: Migration Division, Department of Labor,
Commonwealth of Puerto Rico, November 19, 1953).

Four hundred and sixty years ago today Christopher Columbus
landed on the west coast of Puerto Rico. He and his descendants brought
to us the culture of Spain. We treasure it and maintain it, in a constant
and dynamic adaptation to the modern world and to our job in it. We
are proud of our great literary and artistic tradition and of the deep
feeling for the dignity of the individual which has kept the spirit of the
Spanish people unconquered by foreign invaders or domestic dictators.
This feeling of individualism is a contribution of Spain to modern spiritual democracy, at a time in her history when she no longer makes contribution to political democracy. We are also proud of our close and
fraternal association with the great democracy of the United States.
Being on the frontier of two great cultures has given us an opportunity
to work out a destiny different from, and we believe, better than, the
destiny of millions of people throughout the world in what once were,
or still are, colonies.

On July 25, 1952 we formalized a new relationship between the
people of Puerto Rico and the people of the United States which places
us in a favored position to interpret to the world the true meaning of
liberty and democracy as lived in association by a western Latin people
with the greatest western democracy. On that date we freely associated
ourselves -- through the votes of our people -- with the United States
by a convention mutually binding upon both parties.

We are helping break down some of the old misunderstandings and
suspicions of the economic and political power of the United States,
especially among the 170,000,000 other citizens of the New World in
the 20 Latin-American Republics which also commemorate the daring
voyages of Columbus. I have just returned from several Latin American
countries. I attended the inauguration of President José Figueres of
the Republic of Costa Rica, a great Latin American leader of a great
Latin American democracy, small in territory but large in understanding.
And I can say that the new free relationship between the Commonwealth
of Puerto Rico and the United States is helping to create a better understanding among Latin Americans of the sincerity and devotion of the
people of the United States to the principles of respect for human freedom.

What would Columbus find if he were to return to Puerto Rico
today? As he sailed toward the busy port of San Juan he probably would
be most puzzled by the numerous 10 and 15 storey buildings which mark
our skyline. The old Spanish masonry forts which have guarded the harbor since the days of Sir Francis Drake would look familiar to him. He
would see the ships which carry on trade with the United States mainland ports and with hundreds of others throughout the globe. The customs

officials would tell him that every day we buy $1,240,000 worth of goods from the continental parts of the Union making a total of over $450,000,000 a year that Puerto Rico buys from the United States. If he had come during July of this year, he would have seen 1,086 new cars being unloaded on our docks. He would be astounded at the speed with which they go over the 3,000 miles of paved roads of our island, which is still only 35 miles wide and 100 miles long.

Over 2,000 factories producing cement, glass, paper, fertilizers and hundreds of other products would also undoubtedly puzzle Columbus. We would tell him with pride that 1,388 industries had been built in the past 13 years. We would say that 128 new factories will have been opened this year by the end of December. This is only one part of our battle for production which we call "Operation Bootstrap." We would stress that Puerto Rico is participating in the industrial expansion of the United States as a whole in order to support a population of two and a quarter million people on an island with scanty resources. We want not simply to support our population but further to raise its levels of living.

We could tell Columbus about the progress the people of Puerto Rico have made in the past 13 years in increasing their health, wealth and happiness. Many different comparisons could be made to give an idea of that progress but I think expectancy of life is possibly the most meaningful. When Columbus reached our shores, the people of Europe could count on living an average of only 30 years. When the United States came to Puerto Rico in 1898, our life expectancy at birth was about the same as that of Europe four centuries before. It had been slowly raised to 46 years by 1940. During the succeeding 12 years we pushed it up until an average child born in Puerto Rico this year can reasonably expect to live to the age of 61. This is in dramatic and shocking contrast to the situation of about two-thirds of the world's people, who still have the same life expectancy as that of Europe in 1493, when Columbus sailed. Of course, this phenomenal increase in length of life has increased the urgency and multiplied the problems of our economic development program.

How have we lengthened our lives so much in such a short time? Largely by involving the people themselves in the determination of their own destiny. This has enabled us to see the need for better sanitation and more preventive health measures. These are reflected in a drop in the death rate from 18 per 1000 in 1940 to 9 per 1000 in 1952. This, as many of my listeners will be surprised to hear, is lower than the death rate in the continental United States. We have wiped out malaria; we are well on our way to wiping out the world's greatest killer -- tuberculosis. The tuberculosis death rate in 1940 was over five times what it is today. This year, with a rate of around 50 per 100,000 we are coming close to the U.S. rate and we feel that we are on the road to complete abolition of the "white plague."

Basic to all human progress is education of hand and brain. We are spending over 6 per cent of our entire income -- not just of the Government income but of the entire income of our people -- on education; about 4 times as much proportionately as in the United States. Whereas in 1940 50 per cent of our children did not attend school this year less than 30 per cent are so deprived. Our teachers now number 11,000 compared with 6,000 in 1940. Our literacy rate has risen in the same period from 68 to 78 per cent, and we expect to abolish illiteracy completely withing the next six years. We are proud of our three outstanding institutions of higher learning. Our state university has three fine campuses and 12,000 students. We spend $1,300,000 annually on scholarships in hopes of assuring that no intelligent, capable young man or woman who could make a contribution to the future welfare of our people need go without the higher education which would equip them to make that contribution.

Per capita income has more than tripled since 1940. It is now about $400 a year, which may not sound high in the United States. It would sound high to most of the people in the world, because the average for the world does not quite reach $100 per year. Only four of the 20 Latin-American republics surpass us in per capita income and they all have the advantage of a generous endowment of natural resources and a much lower density of population. Puerto Rico has a population density of 650 per square mile.

We try to make up for our lack of resources by using imaginatively what we do have. Many of our visitors are intrigued by one of our water resource developments. We store water on the northern slope of our central mountains where rainfall is plentiful, release it to generate electricity for our new factories, then send it through the mountains by tunnel to irrigate the semi-arid coastal plain. This and other projects have increased our production of electricity over four times in the past dozen years. Puerto Rico now produces more kilowatt hours per capita than any of the 20 Latin American republics.

We are convinced by the full and generous outpourings of new hope and new energy from our people that we are on the right road. The road is long; it is filled with obstacles. Sometimes the efforts seem to need almost superhuman endurance, but the increasing participation of the people themselves give them and their government the strength to push ahead.

Recently we have been heartened by the world-wide attention "Operation Bootstrap" is receiving. More than 1,000 doctors, nurses, agronomists, civil engineers, educators and others who labor in the field of technical assistance in the development of under-developed areas of the world have come in the past few years to observe what we are doing in Puerto Rico. They also help us understand their problems and therefore gain perspective on our own.

We think Columbus, if he were to return today, would understand what we are trying to do. We would explain it to him in the language of Queen Isabela, although we could also explain it in the language of Sir Francis Drake if Columbus had gotten around to learning it by this time. He would see, we believe, that we are explorers, too. Just as he was an explorer in geographic space, we are explorers in the ranges of improving man's stay on earth. We are trying to push ahead the frontiers of man's knowledge. We are trying to apply it not only to making a better living but, what is more important, to making a better life.

We approach our multitudinous problems with courage born of

the knowledge that we have traveled far on the rocky road. We face the future with the faith that man can and does rise above the pettiness of social position, racial differences, and local and personal economic interests to work for the common good.

We believe that not only Columbus would understand. We believe that all Americans to the north and to the south of Puerto Rico, representing the two great cultures that meet and grow friendly in Puerto Rico, -- trail-blazers both in their different ways -- will also understand.

PUERTO RICO'S CONTRIBUTION TO AMERICA'S PROSPERITY

From Joseph Monserrat, <u>Puerto Rico's Contribution to America's Prosperity: An Address Before the Conference on Automation, Education and Collective Bargaining</u> (San Juan: Migration Division, Department of Labor, Commonwealth of Puerto Rico, December 6, 1963).

For the past two days we have been focusing our attention upon the multiple and complex problems inherent in and the awe-inspiring development of the offspring of man's creative genius -- "Automation." We have been given a splendid and rather unique opportunity to discuss this subject from the myriad backgrounds of the participants and discussants who have been brought together from many countries and fields of endeavor.

We have brought with us our different points of view as to how we can best guide automation -- this precocious child of man's mind -- so that as he grows to full maturity he can fulfill the great promise we see in him. For indeed his promise is great. It is no less a promise than the uplifting of all men everywhere to their full measure of dignity by eliminating want and privation -- the major causes of man's degradation.

We must and indeed do thank the sponsors of this conference for having given us the opportunity to share our knowledge and our thoughts, to pool our ideas so that we might guide our prodigy toward the fulfillment of his promise lest we find we have created a horrendous frankenstein monster who could sharply augment the gulf between the haves and have-nots to a degree that could result in utter chaos.

We Puerto Ricans are indeed honored and privileged that Puerto Rico was chosen as the site for this conference. I sincerely believe that Puerto Rico's recent history can make a modest but nonetheless important contribution to our discussions. I feel a particular personal pride in the role that has been assigned to me, the subject of "Puerto Rico's Contribution to America's Prosperity."

Throughout this conference and from many other sources you have heard of the great advances that have been made in Puerto Rico during the past two decades. However, statistical comparisons alone cannot give us a complete comprehension of the full meaning of these statistics. Let me therefore try to paint a word picture of the problems which faced Puerto Rico some twenty years ago and thus perhaps enable us to appreciate completely the progress made to date and perhaps understand more fully the contributions that Puerto Rico is making to American prosperity.

Some twenty years ago the Chancellor of the University of Puerto Rico, Don Jaime Benitez, devised what might be called a formula to describe to our fellow citizens in the States the all but completely hopeless position that Puerto Rico found itself in at the close of World War II.

With my own embellishments, using Don Jaime's concept, let me describe the problems facing the Puerto Rico of the 1940's.

Puerto Rico is an island 100 miles long and 35 miles wide. In 1940 our density of population was about 544 persons per square mile. We have no subsoil resources. We were a one-crop economy with less than one-half acre of arable land per person on which to grow the food and fiber to feed, house and clothe our constantly growing population. To duplicate in the States the conditions facing Puerto Rico in 1940 (and to some extent still facing Puerto Rico today), we would have to stretch our imaginations to the limit.

The United States is one of the most highly industrialized nations on earth. Puerto Rico, on the other hand, was just beginning to crawl toward industrialization. To resemble Puerto Rico, therefore, we would have to imagine the United States divested of all its industry.

The United States is rich and abundant with subsoil resources. Puerto Rico has no natural resources. Therefore, we would have to imagine the United States with no natural resources.

Puerto Rico has less than one-half acre of arable land per person. The United States, on the other hand, has over four acres of arable land per person. So, imagine if you can, the United States with a half-acre of land per person on which to grow its food and fiber. Not for the population of the United States in 1940 -- nor even for its population of today, but a much, much larger one. How large? Puerto Rico had a density of population of approximately 544 persons per square mile as compared with a density of population of 44.2 persons per square mile in the United States in 1940. In order for the United States to have a density of population equal to the 544 per square mile in Puerto Rico, we would have to imagine that all of the people of Europe, Asia, Africa, Latin America, in short, every single living soul in the world -- one billion seven hundred million persons in 1940 -- lived within the borders of the then forty-eight states.

In short, if we in the United States wanted to understand the problems that Puerto Rico faced in the 1940's, we would have to imagine the United States mainland with all of the peoples of the world crowded into its confines, devoid of its industry, and having no natural resources.

In 1940, Puerto Rico was faced with the three major problems facing most of the peoples of the world. We were an underdeveloped, overpopulated, colonial area.

Today, some 23 years later, I can stand before you and state that the 2,400,000 American citizens residing in the Commonwealth of Puerto Rico are making an important and sizeable contribution to the prosperity of the United States. In 1962, Puerto Rico bought over $930 million worth of goods from the continental United States, making it the fifth largest purchaser of United States goods in the world -- preceded only by Canada, Japan, West Germany, and the United Kingdom.

On a per capita basis however, Puerto Ricans today are by far the best United States customer, purchasing $400 worth of goods per person. Canadians purchase $211 per person, the Dutch $65 and the Venezuelans $62. Perhaps we can more fully understand the meaning of this purchasing power by presenting the facts -- thusly.

Puerto Rico now purchases more United States goods than the South American East-Coast countries Brazil, Uruguay, Argentina and Paraguay.

Puerto Rico also purchases more from the United States than all the South American West-Coast countries Chile, Bolivia, Peru, Ecuador and Columbia.

We now purchase more United States goods than all the six Central American republics together with all the Caribbean islands.

Puerto Rico buys more from the United States than the combined purchases of Spain, Sweden, Denmark, Norway, Austria, Finland, Portugal and Eire.

Our purchases from the United States today are roughly the same as as the total purchases of all of Africa including the United Arab Republic.

If our present growth rate continues, it can be expected that Puerto Rico's purchases from the United States may well equal those of West Germany and Great Britain by 1964.

The following table presents a breakdown of United States exports for 1962 together with population estimates and per capita purchases. It should be noted that for the purposes of this paper I have used the more conservative figure of $930 million instead of the $958 million figure estimated in this table. Also included in the table are the combined total purchases of Latin American countries as well as countries of the African continent and selected European countries.

U.S. EXPORTS FOR 1962

Destination	Amount[1] (in thousands of $)	Population[2]	Per Capita Purchases
Canada	$3,829,715	18,600,000	$211
Japan	1,413,840	94,000,000	15
West Germany	1,075,942	56,200,000	19
United Kingdom	1,074,787	52,700,000	21
PUERTO RICO	958,000[3]	2,400,000	400
Mexico	790,166	36,100,000	22
Italy	767,462	50,400,000	15
Netherlands	752,192	11,700,000	65
India	668,842	440,300,000	1.7

1. Figures by U.S. Department of Commerce
2. Source: World Almanac, 1963
3. Source: Economic Development Administration of Puerto Rico

Destination	Amount (in thousands of $)	Population	Per Capita Purchases
France	585,360	46,200,000	13
Venezuela	468,267	7,500,000	62
Belg/Lux	448,059	9,400,000	48
Brazil	424,804	70,800,000	6
Australia	399,873	10,600,000	38
Argentina	374,513	20,000,000	19

Total six Central American republics	$345,266
Total six Central American republics plus Caribbean islands	763,947
Total Brazil, Argentina, Uruguay, Paraguay	851,617
Total Chile, Bolivia, Peru, Colombia, Ecuador	657,904
Total 13 Latin American republics[4]	939,885
Total African countries (incl. U.A.R.)	979,883
Total eight European countries[5]	940,179

Let us briefly analyze what the $930 million worth of goods shipped from the United States to Puerto Rico means in terms of jobs and income to the various regions of the United States.

From these shipments no less than 42 states benefited directly to the tune of about $485 million in gross income, and further by the employment of approximately 60,000 workers. Forty-six states as well as the District of Colombia benefited indirectly as suppliers of goods and services and derived a total gross income of $435 million. A total of 65,000 workers were employed to provide these different services.

In other words, for every million dollars worth of goods purchased by Puerto Rico, approximately 130 jobs are generated.

In addition, since all but a tiny fraction of all shipments made to Puerto Rico from the United States must by law be shipped in American ships or airplanes, the United States benefits further by about $70 million

4. Peru, Chile, Dominican Republic, Uruguay, Ecuador, Bolivia, Paraguay, Guatemala, El Salvador, Honduras, Nicaragua, Costa Rica, Panama

5. Spain, Sweden, Denmark, Norway, Austria, Finland, Portugal, Eire.

gross income. But this is still not all that needs to be taken into account if we are to fully recognize Puerto Rico's contribution to United States prosperity. We are all aware of the fact that the expenditure of money has a "multiplier" effect; "pump priming" is a familiar phrase used to explain this concept. Thus, when the workers who produced the products Puerto Rico buys spend the $600 million of salaries, wages and profits; and the industries spend some of the $100 million in cash flow; and the $200 million worth of taxes are respent; and then all of these funds are spent again and again, it has been estimated that another $900 million gross income is generated. Thus by using an admittedly conservative "multiplier" of "2", we can say that Puerto Rico's purchases from the United States are directly responsible for two billion dollars of United States gross product.

Every state in the United States mainland derives benefits from Puerto Rico's purchases. The Northeastern States, the North Central States and the South benefit more or less equally from their sales to Puerto Rico. The Northeast receives slightly higher income, while the South gets more jobs. The North Central region is second in terms of income while the Northeast follows the south in job benefits.

The State of New York receives a total of $100 million from purchases made by Puerto Rico and is thus the single largest beneficiary of Puerto Rico's purchases, benefiting further by the generation of 12,000 jobs. It is further interesting to note that Puerto Rico is the second largest customer of the port of New York. Each year some 800,000 tons of products to and from Puerto Rico pass through this port. Only Japan, which is responsible for the movement of 1.5 million tons, surpasses Puerto Rico.

Second to New York is California which receives benefits amounting to some $75 million and 8,500 jobs. Other states which receive significant benefits as a result of Puerto Rico's purchases include Connecticut, Illinois, Massachusetts, Michigan, New Jersey, North Carolina, Ohio, and Pennsylvania.

But, direct purchases from the Commonwealth are not the only contributions that Puerto Ricans make to America's prosperity. Time and space do not permit a detailed analysis of other means through which Puerto Rico contributes to the United States economy. Let me, however, give you two brief illustrations of what I mean.

New York City has a Puerto Rican population of somewhere in the neighborhood of 650,000. There are only 14 cities in the United States whose population is greater than 650,000 inhabitants. Such cities as Pittsburg, Cincinnati, and Buffalo have populations of 604,332 and 502,550 and 532,759 respectively.

This many people obviously represents an important source for the purchase of goods and services which in turn generates jobs. While we do not have accurate figures available, we in the Migration Division of the Commonwealth of Puerto Rico's Department of Labor have made a "guess'timation" that the Puerto Rican population of New York earns a minimum of somewhere in the neighborhood of $525,000,000 a year of which some $90,000,000 are paid in direct and indirect taxes and the balance for the purchase of goods and services. While I do not vouch for the complete accuracy of these figures, it must be obvious to all, that the thousands of Puerto Ricans who work in the garment, service, and manufacturing industries of New York, as well as in the clerical and professional fields, would clearly generate greater income than the cost of public services their physical presence creates for governmental entities.

In the State of New New Jersey over the past 11 years, some 71,000 agricultural workers from Puerto Rico have helped harvest crops worth $754,000,000. We could add to these figures the fact that each year some 14,000 Puerto Rican agricultural workers migrate from Puerto Rico to help harvest crops in more than 13 states.

In the business and professtional world "good will" is an important, valuable and necessary asset for a successful business. In the world of government and governments "good will" and understanding are the major business of Foreign Offices and State Departments throughout the countries of the world. Almost unknown to the vast majority of Americans, the Commonwealth of Puerto Rico is a valuable partner and a major asset to the United States in its dealings with that large part of the world that is called underdeveloped. Its increasingly active role as both a model and teacher to men from Asia, Afica, Latin America and the Near East is probably much better known in Bolivia, Nigeria, India or Iraq than it is in the United States. But known or not, Puerto Rico does make a contribution in this "good will" field which is important to the United States, to the thousands of foreign officials and technicians from over 100 different countries, and to Puerto Rico itself.

I indicated at the outset of this presentation that I believed that Puerto Rico's recent history has a modest, but in my opinion, important contribution to make to our discussions here.

This contribution is not, unfortunately, in the form of specific answers to any of the many specific problems which automation presents, and with which we have been dealing. Rather, I believe our contribution has to do with the manner in which we might seek the solutions to the problems that face us.

The Puerto Rico of today is not the one-crop Puerto Rico of 1940. The people of Puerto Rico today include thousands of individuals who composed the people of Puerto Rico in 1940. But while in a physical sense they may still be the same individuals, they most certainly are not the same people. Our people are healthier, better educated, better housed, better dressed, and above all we are no longer without hope -- for we know that the power to help ourselves lies within us.

Our problems, and there are many, are still far from being solved. We have, however, come a long way in a short time. We have learned much.

Perhaps the greatest lesson that we have learned and are constantly in the process of re-learning, is that we have within ourselves the ability to devise as many solutions to a given problem as our minds can create. Man can do much better than to seek only this or that answer. It does not have to be this or that. There can be a third, a fourth, or as many other answers as our imaginations can create.

From the beginning we learned to differentiate means from ends. Thus, our industrialization program is not, and has never been, an end in and of itself for itself. It has been the means to an end. It has been the means of providing a better economic life for our people. But providing a better economic life is also but a means.

It is a means of enabling our people, once free from the degrading need to literally spend all of their time and all of themselves "scratching for a living," to fully recognize their true worth as human beings; to learn to enjoy life for the joy of living. For our religion has taught us that God's greatest creation was Life, and if we are to venerate God we must venerate his creations -- the greatest of which is Life. For this reason then, man must be the master of his own creations, not their slave.

Automation is a creature of man's creation. We have met here because while we recognize that this, our creature, can add to the meaning and enjoyment of life, by eliminating drudgery and providing greater abundance, we also recognize that the blessings of this creation can indeed be mixed.

Therefore, in all of our planning we must be determined and not permit ourselves to become the slaves of our own creation, but rather, that our creation will serve us even as we serve Him who created us.

THE HISTORY OF THE MIGRATION

From The Puerto Rican Community Development Project
(New York: Puerto Rican Forum, 1964), pp. 10-25.

Each day Puerto Ricans arrive at Kennedy International Airport
by the tens, by the hundreds, to seek their fortune in New York. For most
of them this is the great adventure of their lifetime, the moment toward
which they have saved, struggled and dreamed. They stream off the planes
from San Juan in their clean, best clothes bringing with them a host of new
ideas, a different language, a distinct way of perceiving life, family,
authority, racial issues and human value -- they bring with them a variety
of cultural patterns which in many instances are certain to strike sparks
in the society to which they come. They are young people, alert and eager
for a new and better life for themselves and their children. They are
persevering people who have worked hard and long to earn the fare for the
trip to New York. They arrive in the glittering city anticipating opportunity
for security and advancement. They are white, black and all shades in
between. They often carry with them the name of a friend or a relative
who will assist them with lodging and who will aid them in their search
for employment. They journey over 1,600 miles of ocean to melt into the
life of the city and in many cases become a part of its statistics on poverty.

This profile of the Puerto Rican migration in the mid 1960's in
many ways is similar to the earlier waves of migration, which virtually
wrote the history of the city. There is a letter dating from the year 1626
on file in the Government Archives of The Hague, The Netherlands, stating
that, " . . . the ship the Arms of Amsterdam sailed from New Netherland
out of the Mauritiis (Hudson) River on September 23; they report that
our people there are of good courage and live peaceably. Their women
also have borne children there, they have bought the island Manhattes
from the wild men for the value of sixty guilders . . . "

Thereafter the flow of newcomers to Manhattan's shores never
slackened. The Dutch were followed by the English, Swedes, Norwegians,
Negroes, Jews, Mennonites, Huguenots, Mohammedans. The City's cosmopolitan character was established as early as 1664, when eighteen
languages were said to be spoken. The early migrants were for the most
part successful merchants, traders, craftsmen, aristocrats -- men in
search of their individual fortunes or fleeing from religious persecution
or political difficulties back home. However in the first quarter of the
nineteenth century the pattern began to resemble more closely the migrations that we see today. Whole peasant populations surged into New
York, driven by famine, landlessness. They entered New York without
resources or skills . . . the Irish and the Germans in the first half of
the century, followed by the Italians, the Scandinavians, the Austrians
and the Russian Jews. After the Civil War a great internal migration
of Southern Negroes added to the flow. To all of these the city held out

the hope of freedom, wealth, jobs, education, and personal dignity. But for many of them the bitter harvest was poverty, failure, loneliness, and social ostracism. Epidemics, crime, juvenile delinquency, poverty, drunkenness, were rampant and riots occasionally broke out between ethnic groups. Everything evil in the city was blamed on the newcomers. They were held responsible for degrading neighborhoods and forcing the "respectable" residents out. The newcomers were brutally victimized by greedy landlords and overzealous businessmen. The migrants had no alternative but to pay unreasonably high rentals for rat-infested, poorly equipped housing. They were the constant pawns of disreputable businessmen.

After the First World War, European immigration virtually came to an end due to the combined impact of the new immigration laws and the depression that began in 1929. During the depression "migration" in America came to mean the movement of dispossessed laborers and landless farmers seeking food and work. There was some immigration to New York from Nazi-dominated lands in the 1930's and later, from Communist-dominated countries, but by far, the greatest number of migrants were negroes and Puerto Ricans.

For the Negroes as for the Puerto Ricans the journey to New York was often motivated by a quest for employment. One significant difference must be emphasized. To the Southern Negro the North represented the hope of greater equality and human dignity; to the Puerto Rican equality and human dignity were his birthright . . . only in New York did he tend to forfeit them. In many ways the Puerto Rican migration is analogous to the great European population movements of a century ago. It also bears many striking differences, and these differences and their ramifications, must be explored in order to gain some insight into why the Puerto Ricans in New York have found their stay such an arduous one.

In historical terms, the Puerto Rican migration began, as so many others did, with a slow trickle of craftsmen and merchants in the early part of the nineteenth century. By 1838 there was already a Spanish Benevolent Society formed by Puerto Rican merchants in New York. After 1898, when the United States took Puerto Rico from Spain, the number of Puerto Rican migrants somewhat increased. The two earliest Puerto Rican "neighborhoods" in New York were a small settlement of cigar makers on the lower East Side, and a small group of sailors and their families in the Navy Yard section of Brooklyn. Early census figures show Puerto Ricans living in 39 states and Hawaii by 1910, and in 44 states by 1920. Thereafter, most of the newcomers tended to settle in New York. The percentage of mainland Puerto Ricans residing in New York was 88 percent in the 1940's, and even now, despite efforts on the part of Puerto Rican and American governments to encourage dispersion throughout the country, about 70 percent of the Puerto Rican arrivals remain in the city.

Conditions on the island, too, were changing. From the earliest days of the Spanish settlement, the island's economy had been agrarian. The growing of sugar, coffee, and tobacco dominated island life, and the best lands were used for this purpose, while the growing of food crops for the islanders' use was shunted aside. The tobacco industry, rooted in the popularity of cigars, suffered a grave setback in the 1920's, when cigarettes took over the world market. Fine Puerto Rican coffee, too, was dealt a death blow by a combination of World War I and unfavorable United States tariffs.

The one remaining major crop, sugar cane, was also threatened by competition from Cuba and other sugar-growing islands in the Caribbean, as well as from the beet-sugar growers in continental America. In the 1940's nearly everything the island produced was exported -- sugar, tobacco, rum, needlework -- and its population was poor, dependent, and in despair.

Furthermore the island was drastically over-populated. The continuing high birth rate combined with longer life expectancy because of improved health and sanitary conditions, had, by the 1940's, created a situation where the island simply could not support all her children, for many the alternatives were starvation or migration.

As a result, large numbers of Puerto Ricans began to arrive in New York. In the peak year of the decade, 1946, 39,911 Puerto Ricans entered the United States. Their numbers continued to rise in the 1950's to a high of 69,124 in 1953, dropped sharply with the recession in that year to 21,531 in 1954, then rose again to as high as 52,315 in 1956.

The pattern since has shown a declining migration, at times dropping so far that in 1961 the number of departing migrants exceeded the number of arrivals. However, the flow has subsequently resumed, the number remains high, and the migration is anything but over. At present there are some 260,000 native-born Puerto Ricans and their children living in the United States outside New York City and more than 600,000 within it. These figures rival those of the great European migrations of a century ago, representing more than 25 per cent of the total population of the island. There is yet another facet to the story: each year since the war some 30,000 Puerto Rican farm laborers have come on contract to work in the United States during the harvest season and then to return to the island.

What force moves this tremendous number of human beings across 1,600 miles of ocean to mainland America? The success of Operation Bootstrap -- a wide-range government plan to help the people of the island lift themselves "by their bootstraps" to a better way of life -- has been impressive, and, ironically, this success has intensified the problems of overpopulation and underemployment with which the islanders have been grappling for centuries. In 20 years they managed to cut the average death rate by two-thirds, to alomost double the average life span; a Puerto Rican in 1940 could expect, according to statistics, to live 46 years -- he now can look forward to 70. Great efforts have been made not only to lengthen lives, but to enrich them as well.

Whole communities have pitched in to rebuild their homes and, with government guidance, to build schools for their children, new roads and community centers. Government funds and technical assistance have been combined with local energy and idealism to raze city slums and build apartment developments, start nursery schools, educate and enlighten the adult population as well as the children, and feed their hunger for cultural enrichment with films, books, discussion groups, and foster

a renaissance in Puerto Rican art, music, literature, and folkways.
     With all of this, the government has also set about creating a more
realistic economy. It has tried to break the old dependency on the vagaries
of the sugar-cane market and introduce new industries, both local and
United States-owned, and encourage a growing tourist trade. The achievements have been enormous, and "Operation Bootstrap", "Operation
Serenity", (an effort to overcome the negative results of industrialization)
and the current analysis phase, "The Purpose of Puerto Rico", continue
to animate and inspire life on the island. But the day when Puerto Rico
can offer enough jobs to support all of her people is still painfully remote.
And so the Puerto Rican today finds himself in the ironic position of having
to leave his island, where life, in so many ways, is better than it has
ever been, because he simply cannot make enough money to live there.
     Though the desire for better jobs is by far the most ubiquitous
motive for the journey to New York, there are many other reasons why
the migration continues.
     Many of the newcomers who arrive in New York are not the old,
or the middle class, or the settled folk; they are the young and daring,
willing to pull up their roots and go -- an act which perhaps takes more
courage on the part of the Puerto Rican, with his close home-town and
family ties, than on the part of many other newcomers arriving in this
country.
     Better opportunities for one's family cannot be minimized as a
reason for making the journey. Although educational facilities have been
greatly expanded on the island, schooling in the United States is given
as a reason for migrating. The migrant is also aware of the discrepancy
in salary levels for equivalent jobs on the mainland and at home, and
he dreams of being able to give his family the material comforts that
he knows to be within the reach of even the modest middle class family
in the United States . . . comforts which would be impossible in his own
island.
     Like many immigrants of an earlier period in history, a large num-
ber of Puerto Ricans come to the United States to work and save money
in the hope that they can return to their homes -- and in a far better
financial condition than when they left. The fact that so few manage to
extricate themselves from the city once they are here, does not seem
to deter the young men who keep arriving, full of hope, only to eke out
their existence in a furnished room or with a relative while they try,
usually in vain, to save up enough capital to return to their island in
truimph.
     Puerto Ricans on the island have been saturated with stories about
New York. They have seen it depicted on television and in the movies,
and read about it in the newspapers and in books. Some of them have
been to to the city, and nearly all of them have a friend or relative in
New York who has written or paid a visit home and told them about it.
Despite the fact that some of the stories are stories of defeat, each
newcomer feels that for him it will be different. The very real attractions
that New York has -- good schools, relatives here who will give one a
start, the possibilities of better jobs and better pay -- outweigh, time
and again, the equally real problems that it poses for the migrant.

All of these reasons for coming to New York were, of course, factors in the European migrations, too, and there are many parallels between the nineteenth-century immigrants and the Puerto Ricans who arrive every day at Kennedy Airport. The Europeans, too, bore the burden of poverty, poor housing, and rejection. The Europeans, too, knew disappointment and disillusionment. The irony of the Puerto Rican's situation, however, is that he has not come to escape -- as so many Europeans did -- oppression, discrimination, or breakdown of his society; he has, in fact, come to it.

For most Puerto Ricans, life in New York is their first contact with a social system that puts them on the very bottom rung of the ladder. This fact alone explains much about the Puerto Ricans' bewilderment with the ways of this city. On his island the Puerto Rican is a free citizen -- poor, perhaps, but free and with dignity -- not only a Puerto Rican citizen, but also an American citizen, with all the rights and responsibilities that this involves. In New York, however, he quickly discovers that he must bear the burden not only of being a "foreigner", but also of being considered a "Negro".

New Yorkers seem unaware of the Puerto Rican's rich cultural heritage, dating back to a century before this city was founded. New Yorkers are not cognizant of the fact that to the Puerto Rican his racial heritage is neither a subject of shame nor of particular pride -- simply a fact.

There are yet other ironies. When the nineteenth century Italian, Irishman, or German came searching for a job, he nearly always found one. There was a great demand for unskilled labor -- to build the railroads, dig the canals, man the factories, sail the ships, settle the western lands. But the Puerto Rican immigrant of today has no such opportunities. An advanced technology is eliminating the need for jobs that muscle alone can accomplish. The Puerto Rican is frequently an unskilled worker and is unable to secure employment. His wife may operate a sewing machine or make plastic flowers in a factory; his daughters may get jobs as salesgirls or clerical workers, but he, the head of the family, who by custom, has always been the family provider, accustomed to making the important family decisions, of shaping the destinies of his wife and children -- he can find no employment. Frequently he must remain at home and tend to the tasks which in another age would have been assigned to his wife. His search for employment is answered by rejection after rejection. Moreover his prospects for the future offer little hope for alleviating his destitute condition; the number of available unskilled jobs shrinks daily. The grave consequences to the Puerto Rican migrant, not only in terms of economics, but also in respect to family solidarity, are incalculable.

This great disparity between the values the Puerto Rican brings with him to New York and the realities that are forced upon him by the city lies at the heart of the fate that so often overtakes him . . . the Puerto Rican is an individual . . . not a blank piece of paper awaiting the stamp of the city's rules and regulations. The Puerto Rican is a complete human being with a language, a culture, a way of perceiving life that date back centuries; he comes with a knowledge of his place in in the universe, of his duties to himself, his family, to authority, to God; he comes with a morality, a belief in his own innate dignity as a man and as a member of the human race. And nearly everything that he believes in and cherishes is threatened by the conflicts he encounters in the city.

He cannot accept the concept that race is a barrier to economic achievement. Early in his stay in the big city he learns that the Puerto Rican is often denied employment open to "others," treated with disrespect, refused housing, looked upon by both his black and white neighbors with suspicion and distrust. This comes as a sobering and disillusioning realization.

In Puerto Rico, the mores of the family are strictly delineated and are scrupulously observed. A father is the unquestioned head of the family, accorded respect by his wife and children. He provides for them, furnishes the home, supervises their activities, offers them security and leadership. Second in magnitude to the racial issue confronting the Puerto Rican in New York is the plight of the Puerto Rican male.

The lines of kinship in Puerto Rico are spread generously; life is shared with aunts, cousins, relatives by marriage, neighbors, godparents, friends. No matter how little a family may possess, its members never hesitate to share with a less fortunate relative. This family closeness, with its concomitant warmth and generosity, cushions the harsher aspects of life for the islander. If mothers must work, their children are cared for by loving hands. If a father loses his job, there is a relative who will help the family over hard times. If a person is too old and ill to take care of himself, he need never fear that he will be abandoned.

In New York, the Puerto Rican tries to keep up the strength of this family circle, but there are many things going against him. The American ethic, quickly apprehended, is "fend for yourself" -- and the many pressures of wrestling a livelihood from the hostile, hurried, overpowering city tend to harden a person's sensitivity to the needs of others. The salary dollar, so laboriously earned, must be spread out over so many more necessities of life than in Puerto Rico. Life in an already overcrowded apartment is not so easy to share as life in one's own small house where, whatever the shortcomings, there is all of the outdoors to live in all day, every day. Then, too, the whole circle of family is so geographically spread out, that the whole burden of supporting a newcomer or a relative who is out of work now may fall on one member, where before it would have been shared. It is little wonder that the warmth of family relationships may cool somewhat in the rougher New York climate, and the cushion that the family provided against the shocks and disappointments of the outside world may wear thin. Still, an effort is generally made to retain some semblance of the family circle, and it is a rare newcomer who cannot look forward to a place to stay, at least for a while, and some help, however limited, in finding a job and learning the ways of the city.

Earlier immigrants were sustained and strengthened in their battle with the city by their national protective societies -- the B'nai B'rith, the Irish Emigrant Society, the Croatians and Slovenian Benevolent Societies, the National Order of the Sons of Italy, the Ancient Order of

Hibernians, the Hebrew Immigrant Aid Society. These functioned somewhat like "super" family circles; they might give charity, arrange burials,
create a social life, publish a newspaper, exert political and social
pressure for their members, protect and pass on the traditions and
memories of the old country, preserve the language, the music, and the
handcrafts, keep alive the pride and the independence of their countrymen,
function as unions, political clubs, counselors, employment agencies,
insurance companies, banks, translators, "family." At least partly because of the supportive influence of these societies, the successive im-
migrations to the city achieved a certain social cohesion and strength
and often attained great political impact. The Puerto Ricans in New York
have only started to form such groups.

On Sunday in New York one can wander into hundreds of "home-
town club" meetings, where members gather from every part of the city
to spend their leisure day together, eating, playing cards, making plans
for future activities, or talking over old -- and new -- times. These and
other similar groups have helped the family in its role to cushion the
individual in the face of adversity. There are many church clubs that
have various extra-religious functions, a small number of private social
agencies, and federated citizens' groups. But none of these, has the kind
of encompassing, cohesive power over the total group that the earlier
immigrant societies did. Much of the material help offered by these
societies of the earlier immigrants is now given by agencies, but there
still remain functions which such groups perform which can only be
performed by the groups themselves. In most cases the agencies cannot
communicate with the Puerto Rican because they have no knowledge of
his language or the mores of the group.

For the Puerto Rican, with his background of male dignity, taking
welfare money is an admission to the world that he is a failure as a man,
a husband, and a father; it shames and humiliates him; the acceptance
of these token monies creates deeper and more corrosive problems than
it solves.

One of the great anomalies of the Puerto Rican migration arises
out of the special curcumstances of our age, in which the voyage, literally
between two worlds, can be accomplished in three hours. The Puerto
Rican from the country goes in three hours, out of a life virtually un-
changed from the nineteenth century village life the Spaniards founded
when they populated the island, into a space-age New York. Although
the Puerto Rican arriving from the city is perhaps more prepared for
this encounter there is nevertheless a "time travel" quality to his journey.
Not unlike the European immigrants he is skilled in operations that require of him strength, willingness to work, patience, ability to take orders.
But unlike them the new migrant is faced with a paucity of jobs, and those
available do not require what he has to offer. He finds that there is only
a market for skilled, professional and white collar workers who seem
to have an exclusive priority to all of the things that he desires. The
affluence of the city magnifies his poverty and only contributes to make
his life, on a mere subsistence level, almost unendurable.

Some who achieve financial success move away from the city to melt
comfortably into the milieu of suburbia. There are those who gain a
foothold in the entertainment world, in politics, sports and the professions,

and those who have achieved seniority and skill at their jobs. Others have had their most cherished dream of sending their children through college and on to a professional career realized. And there are some who sustain their goal of returning to the island, and manage to return with their families and establish business there.

In contrast to the labored gains of the Puerto Rican in New York, Glazer and Moynihan note in their book, Beyond the Melting Pot, that Puerto Ricans who migrated to St. Croix of the Virgin Islands, have distinguished themselves as "economically successful".

However, despite the attainments of the Puerto Ricans in the history of their migration to the city, studies reveal that half of the group has been caught in the inexorable cycle of poverty. It is tragic for the city of New York, that so many of the Puerto Ricans who have come in search of a better life have found instead slums, poverty, inadequate education, the destruction of cultural patterns and absence of viable substitutes, exploitation, and meager incomes.

The factual substantiation for these conditions has long been hidden by the claim that the situation would resolve itself in the near future as the numerous services and millions of dollars spent by public welfare would begin to take effect.

PUERTO RICAN MIGRATION: THE IMPACT ON FUTURE RELATIONS

> From Joseph Monserrat, "Puerto Rican Migration: The Impact on Future Relations," (New York: Department of Labor, Migration Division, Commonwealth of Puerto Rico, 1968); also in <u>Symposium: Puerto Rico in the Year 2000</u> (Washington: Howard University Press, 1968).

Future relations between Puerto Rico and the United States are fairly clear on at least one point -- there will be a permanent form of association between the two countries. Results of the 1967 plebiscite demonstrate beyond question that the Puerto Rican electorate desires permanent association. With 66 per cent of the eligible voters participating, 99 per cent of them voted for permanent union. Of these, 60 per cent voted for continuing Puerto Rico's Commonwealth Status, although in an improved form. Thirty-nine per cent wanted Puerto Rico to become a State.

Judging from the results of the plebiscite and from recent elections, independence -- separation from the United States -- is not a major consideration of the Puerto Rican electorate. As stated in the report of the United States-Puerto Rico Commission for the Study of the Status of Puerto Rico:

> "In 1952, 77 per cent of the people of Puerto Rico voted for their two principal political parties that advocated, although in different forms, a permanent union between Puerto Rico and the United States based upon common U.S. citizenship; and this percentage has since increased steadily with each election, reaching 94 per cent in 1964."[1]

1967 PLEBISCITE

(66.3% of voters participating)

Commonwealth		Statehood		Independence	
No.	%	No.	%	No.	%
425,132	60.4	274,312	39.0	4,248	0.6

---

1 <u>Report of the U.S.-Puerto Rico Commission for the Study of the Status of Puerto Rico,</u> Puerto Rico Booklet No. 5, p. 8.

VOTES POLLED BY PARTIES IN THREE ELECTIONS

(Source: State Board of Elections)

Party	1956	1960	1964
Popular Democratic	433,000	457,880	487,267
Statehood Republican	173,000	252,364	284,639
Independence *	86,000	24,103	22,195
Christian Action *	-------	52,096	26,864

That the people of Puerto Rico, through the plebiscite, have indicated their desire for the future status of Puerto Rico to be a more fully developed Commonwealth, is abundantly clear.

However, as the Status Commission notes:

"One of the virtues of the Commonwealth is the fact that it possesses a flexibility which will permit future changes within itself and which also permits freedom of choice of any alternative status that may be the future mutual desire of Puerto Rico and the United States."

Thus, what may not be clear in the minds of many, despite the obvious results of the plebiscite, is the form that association between the two countries will take. Will it be a more fully developed concept of the Commonwealth based on the existing relations between the two countries, or will it be Statehood?

The Status Commission report and supporting papers detail many of the areas that need study to make of the existing Commonwealth concept the more fully developed, creative and dynamic status its backers believe it to be. To investigate these areas, a number of ad-hoc committees will be appointed. They will make recommendations to both the Governor and the Legislature of Puerto Rico and to the President and the Congress of the United States, on how to deal with legal-constitutional, social-cultural and economic factors that will affect the establishment of a more fully developed Commonwealth.

There are, however, several other factors that will affect future relations between Puerto Rico and the United States to which little attention is being given. These relate to the nature of the United States Puerto Rican population as it is today and as it grows and develops in the future.

For the Puerto Rican experience in the United States will play an important role in shaping the future of the Island. In turn, what happens on the Island will influence the Puerto Rican experience here. There is

---

* The Independence and Christian Action Parties failed
to obtain 10% of the total vote, the requirement for
being considered legal parties.

a dynamic relationship, although it may not be overly apparent, between the two Puerto Rican populations.

Puerto Rico is a growing, dynamic society. Its goals and its direction are still in the making. It looks out on the world for the results of various social and economic experiences. It studies these experiences with a view toward adopting those that appear most appropriate to the needs of its people. Of course, it looks nowhere more closely than it does to the experience of its people in the United States.

On the other hand, Puerto Ricans here, especially a group I will discuss later -- a group I call the New Puerto Ricans -- look back to the Island for the cultural heritage that is the legacy of all Puerto Ricans no matter where they live. This is not a casual look for heritage, but a searching for strength to meet the pressures of life in the States.

Moreover, Puerto Ricans here will play an important role, perhaps even a crucial one, in determining the nature of the Commonwealth status, as discussed above, that is yet to be established. Therefore, they will have a hand in influencing the political, economic and social nature of Island society.

This paper will be devoted to discussing the nature of the Puerto Rican experience in the United States, because that experience will go far in determining the dynamics between the two Puerto Rican populations.

Succinctly stated, what role Puerto Ricans here will play in affecting Puerto Rico's future depends upon two major factors:

> 1) How well informed Puerto Ricans in the States are regarding the realities, needs and desires of their fellow Puerto Ricans in Puerto Rico.
>
> 2) How well informed the Puerto Ricans on the Island are regarding the realities of their fellow Puerto Ricans in the States.

In turn, much of these questions will depend on how Puerto Ricans here grow and develop, based upon the sociological and psychological impact of their experience in the States during the next thirty years.

Therefore, the discussion here will be directed at the three major factors molding Puerto Rican experience in the States. These are:

> 1) The present situation of Puerto Ricans in the United States.
>
> 2) The Puerto Rican experience that stems from migration here.
>
> 3) The influence of American racism on Puerto Ricans.

By gaining a clear understanding of these factors, we will have isolated the most important elements of Puerto Rican life in the United States. Then we can examine how these elements will operate in the dynamics of Puerto Rico's future.

Characteristics of the U.S. Puerto Rican Population

First, it must be remembered that the great majority of Puerto Ricans residing in the United States have lived here for less than 15 years.

Second, almost 50% of the United States Puerto Rican population is under 21 years of age.

Third, among those Puerto Ricans born in the United States of Puerto Rican parents, about 84% are under 14 years of age.

There are presently approximately one million Puerto Ricans residing in the United States.[2] The present estimated population of Puerto Rico is 2,700,000.[3] In other words, of a total 3,700,000[4] Puerto Ricans, some 36 per cent of them live in the States.

By 2000, the population of Puerto Rico, given the present rate of natural increase, will have reached at least 5,000,000 persons. During the same period of time, the Puerto Rican population in the continental United States, based in natural increase alone, will have doubled. It is also reasonable to estimate that the United States Puerto Rican population will have grown at an even faster rate than Puerto Rico's because migration during that period will have continued at a rate no less than its present rate -- about 30,000 persons per year. This is provided of course, that during the next 30 years we will not experience any major recession or depression. Thus, we can estimate that by the year 2,000 there may be 2,000,000 Puerto Ricans residing in the United States, representing 40 per cent of the total Puerto Rican population.

Although we speak of Puerto Ricans as a single group, the reality is that Puerto Ricans in the States constitute at least three different groups. These can be roughly defined as the first generation, the bridge generation, and the second generation.

The first generation is composed of Puerto Ricans born, raised and educated in Puerto Rico. Although they have made adjustments to their new environment, their value system, thought patterns and emotional reactions are still primarily rooted in Puerto Rico, much more so than are the other two groups.

The bridge generation are those Puerto Ricans who were born in Puerto Rico, spent part of their lives and received some of their education in the Commonwealth, but migrated at an early enough age to complete their education in the States. They also have lived in cities for a significant part of their lives, and have acquired and assimilated more of the values, life patterns and emotional reactions of the United States than have members of the first generation.

Because of age and other demographic factors of which I have spoken, the second generation Puerto Rican is not yet as an important segment of the Puerto Rican community in the States as he will be by 2000. It is he that will have an important hand in determining the future relations of Puerto Rico and the United States as well as the nature of Puerto Rican society here and on the Island. To understand how he will grow and develop in the United States we must look to his roots in the United States to isolate the factors that will bear most heavily on his growth. One of the most important of these is his forebearer's experience in the United States. This will be his legacy. And the story of Puerto

---

2. United States Census of the Population, 1960, U.S. Department of Commerce
3. Puerto Rico Planning Board
4. This figure does not include the several odd thousand more Puerto Ricans living in other countries throughout the world.

Ricans here is really the story of their migration and experience here.

Migration Theory

Migration, particularly the Puerto Rican migration to the United States, has been the subject of much concern, study and discussion over the last twenty years. Yet, migration itself is perhaps one of the least understood phenomena in the study of history.

The importance of developing a working theory of migration is great. For such a theory would provide the context in which we could develop a proper view of the situation of the newcomer. Arguments that we hear today such as that the newcomer must undergo the pains that naturally arise from a transitional state would go out the window.

For example, Charles R. Lawrence[5] has said that, "The minority experience is part of the history of virtually every ethnic, national and/or racial group in the United States." It is equally true that " . . . all have known the sting of name-calling devices, the hurts of economic discrimination, and the slight of social exclusion." So true are these statements and so frequently have they been excepted that they have become turismatic clichés. Indeed, for many, they have become something far more sinister. They have become "the explantion," the reason, the conscious salve, or to use the more expressive vernacular -- they have become the "cop-out" that substitutes for understanding minority group experience. We expect group C to be treated thus and so because that is how groups A and B were treated before them. Such a viewpoint stems from a real lack of understanding of newcomers -- be they Puerto Rican or blacks who have recently migrated in large numbers from rural to urban areas. This failure to develop a theory of migration hinders us from developing a workable theory of migration with which we could pinpoint the conditions that hamper or even stymie the newcomer in his new environment. With such a theory we would not have to rationalize our failures by saying that suffering is an inherent condition of migration. Such a rationalization is apparent, as I will soon show, in explanations of the Puerto Rican condition, where the Puerto Rican is seen as a problem rather than as reflecting the existing problems of our cities.

Let us turn now to migration theory and ask what such a theory would have to provide.

Although great mass migrations have occured which have changed the course of history, there is little literature on the theory of the dynamics of migration. We know much of why people leave their homeland and of the reception they receive in their new home. There is even a growing literature on how migrants have changed the course of history. But these factors are usually examined from an overview perspective. We know results but not causes.

Overwhelming questions about migration remain unanswered. For example, what considerations spark migration? Is there a critical point

---

5 Charles R. Lawrence, "Negro Americans and Other Minority Groups".

in the national life after which internal forces precipitate a migration? In chemistry we know that at a critical point the addition of one grain of solute to a solution causes precipitation. Can such a point be isolated for study in national life, such that we can measure the forces at play and predict when the precipitation of people from one nation to another will occur?

These are important questions, one on which the genius of our social scientists should be brought to bear, because there are many dilemmas in the migration question. For example, why is it that the same forces in different nations brings about emigration while in other countries masses sit out bad conditions. Why is it that one period of history witnesses a mass exodus of persons to foreign shores while during other periods there is little or no migration?

These are just some of the unanswered but crucial questions that remain unresolved in our study of societies. Yet, in America -- often called the land of the immigrant, a term that includes the migrant -- there is not one university in which a single course on migration is offered. Nor is there a single basic book with which to teach such a course. Today, when over five million Americans change state residence each year, there is no workable theory of migration nor of its ramifications.

Although it has been said there is no law of migration, because migration is so lawless, those of us directly involved in the Puerto Rican migration have had to seek answers to numerous problems related to the Puerto Rican migration by conceptualizing hypotheses to establish a theoretical framework within which to work.

The Puerto Rican Migration

Puerto Rican migration to the States follows what can be called a "classical pattern," because it is a migration which is primarily economically motivated. Thus, its ebb and flow can be charted and predicted. A basic hypothesis for the Puerto Rican migration to the continent may be stated thusly:

> The size of the Puerto Rican migration varies closely with job opportunities in the United States, i.e., when job opportunities increase, migration increases; when job opportunities decline, migration declines. During depressions more Puerto Ricans return to Puerto Rico from the United States than migrate from Puerto Rico.

The validity of this postulate can be verified by an examination of the available data on Puerto Rican migration.

Since the 1930 census, Puerto Ricans have been counted as living in every state of the Union. However, during the 1940's, 80 per cent of the Puerto Ricans moving to the States settled in New York City, the world's largest labor market. Since then, as new job openings have created increased demand for workers in other areas of the United States, the proportion of those settling in New York has declined steadily and appears to have leveled off at about a little less than 60 per cent of the total annual migration.

Data on Puerto Rican migration to the continental United States demonstrates that the major factor affecting this movement is available job opportunities here. The belief that a drop in net migration to the United States is affected by the growing number of jobs resulting from the industrialization of Puerto Rico cannot be validated by available evidence. In other words, the "pull" factor in migration, i.e., the availability of jobs in the States, is the dominant determination that regulates net migration figures. Conversely, jobs in Puerto Rico resulting from the industrialization program there, as yet, play little, if any role, in influencing migration either to or from Puerto Rico.

Let us examine briefly the reality into which Puerto Ricans enter in the States.

The first "airborne" migration in history began in 1946. Prior to 1946, there were between 50,000 and 75,000 Puerto Ricans living in New York City. There was no "Puerto Rican problem." In fact, being Puerto Rican in New York City was a positive status. Puerto Ricans were sought as good workers. Also, there was no housing shortage during the economic depression that immediately preceded World War II. The neighborhoods in which Puerto Ricans lived were few in number (El Barrio in East Harlem being the principal one), and Puerto Ricans shared the hardships of the depression with their neighbors of various other ethnic backgrounds.

Shortly after the end of the war, the situation began to change. By 1948, the nation and most of the literate world "knew" that New York City had a "Puerto Rican Problem." Newspaper headlines heralded a "New Airborne Invasion" when the regular scheduled and non-scheduled airlines began runs between New York and the Island. Other headlines told of "A New Race of Cave Dwellers" as pictures showed Puerto Rican families living in basements and coal bins. The ashcan school of photography had a field day photographing Puerto Ricans living in slum conditions.

In 1946, out-migration from Puerto Rico equaled 39,911 persons, 95 per cent of whom came and remainded in New York City. At the time, this was the largest out-migration in any one year since records had begun to be kept in 1908. The relatively inexpensive air rates and fast planes helped, but the major reasons for migration were two: there was a backlog of people who had not been able to leave during the blockade days of the war, and there was a great need for workers in New York City due to an upswing in consumer products production. Puerto Rican veterans returning from the war were entering the labor force; they were "looking around" for work and living off the "52-20 Club", as the unemployment insurance program for veterans was called.

The pre-war and war years put an end to the depression. The resulting prosperity set off a chain reaction which is still in motion. For the first time since the depression, low-cost housing, in fact all housing, became scarce. Married children who had "doubled up" and "tripled up" with their parents during the "hard times" now had money to secure their own apartments. Marriages that had been delayed for lack of work were begun and soon the war-baby boom was on. The sense of unity the nation had developed during the war remained, but the enemy had disappeared. However, the newspapers were already presenting New Yorkers with a new "enemy," the Puerto Ricans. History repeated itself. What took place in New York City in 1946-47-48, and is taking place today, had occured often in the past.

Puerto Ricans as Symbols Today

In New York City today Puerto Ricans are a symbol. They symbolize -- indeed personify -- the basic problem of the city. Today, even as one hundred years ago, New Yorkers facing the problems of rapid community changes rarely reason abstractly about the cause of these changes.

Puerto Ricans come to New York because New York has jobs that need to be filled; because New York needs Puerto Ricans. However, because of one of its basic problems -- lack of planning -- New York is no more ready to receive Puerto Ricans now, than it was to receive the immigrants it needed a century ago. New York is not unique. Neither Chicago, Cincinnati, Milwaukee nor any other city is ready to receive the new blood needed to keep it economically healthy and culturally alive.

Therefore, rather than viewing the problems of its Puerto Rican population as reflecting the problems of this country's urban centers, Puerto Ricans are themselves viewed as presenting a problem to the cities. Thus, we have, "The Puerto Rican Problem." This is nothing more than seeing an effect as a cause. It is also a means of developing a scapegoat for the conscience of established groups and interests in the cities.

There is a simple link with what I stated earlier about a proper theory of migration dynamics with what I have stated above. It is that if we properly understood the Migration process, we might be able to arrive at a proper means of viewing newcomers to the city. It would be a means leading us from the path of developing scapegoats to one that would lead us to developing solutions to the problems that plague all residents of our cities. This failure of understanding is not just to be condemned both intellectually and morally, it is also one of the keys toward understanding the reality of present day Puerto Ricans, especially second generation Puerto Ricans. It is they who are nurtured in an atmosphere of being "problems" to the city. It is this stigma that is their reality, as it is the reality of their bridge generation brothers and their first generation fathers. It is in this atmosphere that their minds and hearts are formed. And this will play an important role, as I will later show, in determining how they will view the nature of the relationship between Puerto Rico and the United States, a relationship which I have demonstrated is still to be determined and in which they will have a hand in determining.

There is, another important element in this picture:

American Racism

Racism is inherent in American society. It is an American cultural trait. It is not an aberration, but rather the norm. Early as well as recent American history bears this out. The Founding Fathers, we are taught, came to this country in search of religious and political liberty. What is excluded from the lesson is that they came seeking this liberty for themselves and immediately denied it to others. It must be remembered that the Founding Fathers brought with them to this country the bitter experience of religious and political struggles in Europe, as Vernon Parrington[6] and others have so well documented. They could not help but transplant, with modifications, the lessons of their experience.

Other groups that have come to these shores followed in the Founding Fathers' footsteps, seeking liberty for themselves, but, also seeking to exclude others from obtaining equal rights because they believed equality threatened their liberty, rather than what is really true -- that the extension of freedom makes all men more free.

Today we see the results of this process. We live in a racist society. But we look to the wrong source for the origin of racism. We seek to explain what is regarded as this unusual phenomena in the character of minority groups. We believe that the disease originates in a specific organ rather than realizing that the entire body is shot-through with virulence. When blacks are excluded from the opportunity to advance, we look at the blacks and ask what is wrong with them that they cannot attain the fundamental blessings of American life -- a good job, a good education and a good home. We should ask what is wrong with American life that the blacks cannot attain what others have.

As the recent report of the President's Commission on Riots and Civil Disorders eloquently points out, the riots in the City did not begin in the ghetto tenements, plotted in cellars by several desparate men. They began in the comforts of suburban and urban homes, unconsciously formulated by well-meaning men who see nothing in the adverse conditions they promote, and from which they benefit, that can lead to rioting.

No longer can we look at minority groups and ask what is wrong with them. We must take a piercing look at the majority and ask what in its culture, in its institutions and in its everyday life is so wrong that it incorrectly believes its life can only be perpetuated through the denial of rights and opportunity to others. Then we will be finally coming to grips with what has long been buried in American education and thought -- the ugly spectre of racism.

It is within this spectre of racism in the United States that Puerto Ricans find themselves. No issue will have a greater effect upon the Puerto Rican communities of the States then the present struggle for equality that is so frequently referred to as the Black revolution.

The Puerto Rican Reality

The reality, however, is that this profound social revolution is more than just Black. It involves many groups -- one of these is Puerto Ricans. The Puerto Rican involved in the struggle has

---

6. Vernon Louis Parrington, Main Currents in American Thought, Harcourt, Brace and Company, New York, 1930.

two special problems:

First, although many of his fellow Americans know intellectually that he is a citizen, emotionally he is regarded as a foreigner, with all this term implies for Americans.

Second, and perhaps most important, Puerto Ricans are not a race -- they are an ethnic group in which some members are "white" some "black" and some so-called "mixed".

In other words, in a sense, Puerto Ricans are the only racially integrated group in the United States, as we have come to know the meaning of the word integrated. As such, they suffer the peculiar problem of not being understood either by their black brothers or by their so-called white neighbors.

To black men, Puerto Ricans are trying to "pass". They do not understand why Puerto Ricans have not joined them in a more militant manner in the Civil Rights struggle.

For too many of his white neighbors the Puerto Rican is seen as a non-white person with all that this implies within the American reality. What neither black nor white Americans understand is that Puerto Rico has never had what we in the United States call a minority group. In Puerto Rico the only people who are called a "minority" are those members of political parties that fail to win an election.

Puerto Ricans, therefore, whether black, white or mulatto have not received the same conditioning in this regard as have both the American black and whites.

This is not to imply that there is no prejudice among us Puerto Ricans. However, in our history as a people prejudice has been limited primarily to relations between individuals, and has never been socially instituted. In our history of more than 450 years, we have never had a broad scale system of institutionalized discrimination.

Puerto Ricans, whether black or white, have never had to bear the horrendous burden of fighting those who would make them feel or believe that they were lesser human beings because of skin pigmentation, or for that matter, for any other reason.

There has never been a race riot in Puerto Rico.

This, then, is one of the major differences between the blacks and the Puerto Ricans in the United States: that all Puerto Ricans are not "colored", and that even among those who are, color is not a major issue in Puerto Rican life.

Another significant difference is that Puerto Ricans represent a whole, unlike the blacks, who represent a part or minority of a whole. For this reason, Puerto Ricans are accustomed to seeing other Puerto Ricans at work at all levels, from low-income farm workers to the rich landowner who hire them; from the teacher who teaches them to the head of the University; from the district political leader to the Governor, the members of the Cabinet, and the members of the House and Senate.

I repeat. The Puerto Rican by experience, conditioning and history is not a member of a minority group. He is a part of the whole, and the whole itself -- despite existing differences of class.

The Black Revolution today is first of all a struggle to secure the self respect and dignity due blacks because they are human beings.

This self respect and dignity Puerto Ricans have had for centuries. They have it in Puerto Rico (part of the American Union) and they insist on keeping it wherever they go.

For the Puerto Rican, therefore, particularly for those of the first and bridge generations, his struggle today, and increasingly so in the next thirty years, is and will be to retain the rights he has always had, rather than to attain rights he has never had.

For Puerto Ricans anywhere to accept the values, or more correctly the state of mind that color represents in the United States, would be to introduce into their way of life a racism that has never existed in the form in which it exists in the United States. To accept this racism would mean -- figuratively and literally in some cases -- to split the Puerto Rican family down the middle. This is true today, particularly among the first and bridge generation.

The New Puerto Rican

At this point I would like to speak briefly about the second generation Puerto Rican -- the Puerto Rican born in the States of Puerto Rican parents. I will hereafter call him the new Puerto Rican.

The new Puerto Rican is a phenomenon who might add a new dimention to the concept of pluralistic democracy. Second generations of the past, at great psychic cost, resolved their problems by giving up, in order to become "Americans," the values, culture, religion and sometimes even the name of their parents. It is interesting to note that the United States is one of the few countries of the world where a man can consider himself educated and speak but one language. This, despite the fact, that the United States, perhaps more than any other country in the world, has received thousands of people who have spoken all of the world's languages. It may well come to pass that the new Puerto Rican may break this traditional, historical reality, both for the betterment of American life and its world image as well as for his own psychic salvation.

To understand the new Puerto Rican we must appreciate the fact that to be Puerto Rican in the United States is very different from being Puerto Rican in Puerto Rico. This is particularly true for the new Puerto Rican. He is Puerto Rican because he cannot be anything else. He does not have, as does his father of the first generation and his older brothers of the bridge generation, the knowledge, experience or security of knowing what it is to be a Puerto Rican in Puerto Rico. He has been raised in a setting where he is a minority, where he is different, which in the reality of the United States has always meant to be "less than", i.e., inferior to others.

Unlike his brothers in Puerto Rico, he is not just a child in school; he is a Puerto Rican. He is also something else, When I was being raised in East Harlem, I was frequently called a "spik." I am no longer called a "spik." I am now referred to as being culturally deprived, socially disadvantaged and a product of the culture of poverty. This too, is the reality of the new Puerto Rican.

Furthermore, the new Puerto Rican is an unknown quantity, and an unknown reality to his cousins in Puerto Rico, who because of their conditioning cannot fully understand the peculiar and particular reality of their state-side equivalent.

Although there is much discussion regarding the problem of identity in Puerto Rico, it becomes academic when compared to the identity problem of the new Puerto Rican. No Puerto Rican in Puerto Rico need constantly remind himself that he is Puerto Rican. The new Puerto Rican, on the other hand, must, almost literally remind himself every minute of every day that he is Puerto Rican. If he does not constantly remind himself of this fact, there are many others who will not let him forget it. The dilemma of the new Puerto Rican is that he is most certainly not Puerto Rican in the sense that he would be if he resided in Puerto Rico. He cannot be. The stimuli and values around him as well as the ever-present reality of his minority group position, among other reasons, make this impossible.

Frequently, the new Puerto Rican has never even seen Puerto Rico and quite frequently does not even speak Spanish. But, to all those around him, he is Puerto Rican. And indeed he is -- he is the new Puerto Rican! There are those who, at this time, might point out that second generation groups of the past have also found themselves in similar position, i.e., being neither fish nor foul -- like the new Puerto Rican, neither Puerto Rican in the Puerto Rico sense nor fully American.

There are however, a series of variables that separate the situation of the new Puerto Rican from that of other Puerto Ricans in the United States, and that also hinders understanding among the various groups. One of these is citizenship. The same citizenship status among Puerto Ricans here and on the Island causes a unique dilemma.

As a citizen of the United States, the Puerto Rican born in the Commonwealth of Puerto Rico, a part of the American Union, need never learn English nor lose his cultural identity. He need never become a carbon copy of something he is not. If, however, he were to migrate from one part of the Union -- Puerto Rico -- to another part of the Union, New York City this is exactly what he is expected to do.

That he should learn English, both as a tool for realizing the aspirations that motivated him to leave home, and as a means of expanding his knowledge and to further fulfill himself as a person, needs no discussion. But, at the same time that he is asked to learn English, he is asked to depersonalize himself by giving up the values and culture that give meaning and reality to his life. This is tantamount to a tacit judgement that his culture and values are inferior. He is told by words at times and by inference at other times that the values he holds dear are not worthy of his children. This represents the essence of denigration.

The new Puerto Rican does not fully understand the dilemma of his first generation father and bridge generation uncle. He sees in that which his father represents the cause for his not being accepted as part of the whole and as the reason why he must constantly be reminding himself that he is Puerto Rican although he is not sure what that means.

Puerto Rico and the United States

As I have demonstrated, much of Puerto Rico's future will turn on the relationship that is yet to be established with the United States. A key role in determining this relationship will fall to Puerto Ricans in the United States, especially the new Puerto Rican who by 2000 will compose a major portion of the Puerto Rican population here. His growth will take place within the context of American society. The primary elements that will influence his growth are the migration experience of his father and the legacy of problems stemming from migration that become incorporated into his heritage.

In addition, the American culture, and the racism that runs through it, will also be key factors in determining the new Puerto Rican world view. These factors will naturally color the manner in which he views what is best for Puerto Rico, and therefore, the manner in which he exerts his influence on Congress toward an ultimate solution of Puerto Rico's political status.

Many possibilities exist for how his view of Puerto Rico's situation will be colored. The new Puerto Rican may feel that his suffering is due to being an outsider in America. This may cause him to project a State-hood solution onto Puerto Rico, thinking that through Statehood his problem of being considered an outsider will disappear. He may project an Independence solution, hoping thereby to erase the position of limbo in which he finds himself. Thus through Independence he may attempt to demonstrate to the society that stigmatizes him that he has made his choice.

Finally, he may take the path leading toward a more dynamic Commonwealth status, one that fully realized the hopes of Puerto Ricans on the Island and those here who see in maintaining the link with their birthland a means of gaining strength from their culture to combat the problems they face here.

All these paths are frought with danger because the ultimate status of Puerto Rico should be wrought in the hands of the Puerto Ricans on the Island -- the Puerto Ricans who will be most affected by the status and the ones who are closest to the dynamics of their own society. Only Puerto Rico can judge what solution it wants for itself.

If the bitter experience through which the first generation, bridge generation and the new Puerto Rican pass causes them to project a solution for their situation onto the ultimate solution of Puerto Rico's political status, they will do great harm both to themselves and to their brothers on the Island. They cannot use their political strength in favor of a status solution different from that which their compatriots on the Island wish.

All generations must, therefore, maintain the bonds that the first and bridge generations have with their Puerto Rican brothers on the Island. Only by so doing can they keep each other informed of the realities of the two countries and the differing needs of the Puerto Rican populations. The Puerto Ricans of both countries will gain the necessary resolve through their alliance to help solve each other's problems.

Trying to define the Puerto Rican community in New York City is much more difficult than defining it in Puerto Rico. The Puerto Ricans who were to give the character to the later migration—the poor in search of work—began to settle in New York City during World War I.[1] The first settlement was in the area of the Brooklyn Navy Yard, probably responding to the demand for workers during the war years. About the same time, Puerto Ricans began to settle in Harlem, just as the newly arriving Blacks were settling there. The 1920 census reported 7,364 persons of Puerto Rican birth residing in New York City. Brooklyn Navy Yard and Harlem continued to be areas of settlement during the 1920's. A New York City Health Department Study[2] reported 44,908 persons of

The Puerto Rican Community in New York City *

Puerto Rican birth living in New York City in 1930, an increase of 35,544 during the 1920–1930 decade. By this time, the great majority of Puerto Ricans were settling in Harlem, with 80 per cent of the Puerto Rican population of New York residing there. The Brooklyn Navy Yard section continued to be second, containing 16 per cent of the Puerto Rican population. Figure 5–1 indicates the place of residence of Puerto Ricans in Harlem in 1935; Figure 5–2 indicates the place of residence of Puerto Ricans in Brooklyn in 1935.

Migration slowed during the depression years of 1930–1940. The 1940 census reported 61,463 persons of Puerto Rican birth residing in New York, an increase of 16,555 during the decade. Migration practically stopped during World War II, but after 1945 the rate began to increase rapidly. The population continued to settle in the Harlem and Brooklyn Navy Yard areas, but it flowed over from Harlem to East Harlem, and across the Harlem River into the South

[1]For the details of the early settlement of Puerto Ricans in New York, see Lawrence R. Chenault, *The Puerto Rican Migrant in New York City* (New York: Columbia University Press, 1938), Chaps. 4, 6.

[2]John L. Rice, "Health Problems among Puerto Ricans in New York City," unpublished Report of the Health Department of New York City, 1934. Quoted by Chenault, *ibid.*, p. 58.

* Joseph P. Fitzpatrick, Puerto Rican Americans: The Meaning of Migration to the Mainland, ©1971, pp. 53–72. Reprinted by permission of Prentice-Hall, Inc., Englewood Cliffs, New Jersey.

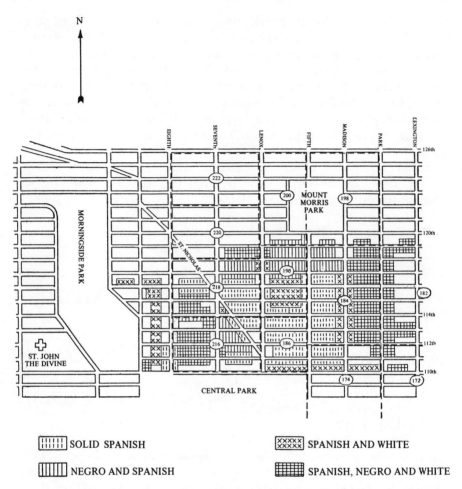

Fig. 5–1. Settlement of Spanish-Speaking Racial Groups in the Lower Harlem Area, New York City, 1935. Classifications of racial groups other than Spanish-speaking are omitted. Census tracts are indicated by broken lines. In the map, language takes precedence over color. Reproduced from Lawrence R. Chenault, *The Puerto Rican Migrant in New York City* (New York: Columbia University Press, 1938), Fig. 2, p. 95 [adapted from a map study prepared by the New York Urban League which appeared in the *Sun*, March 22, 1935, in *The New York Times*, March 24, 1935, and in James Ford, Katherine Morrow, and G. Thompson, *Slums and Housing* (Cambridge, Mass.: Harvard University Press, 1936), I, 323], by permission of Columbia University Press.

Bronx. From the Brooklyn Navy Yard the population pushed northeast into Williamsburg. Figure 5–3 traces the spread of the Puerto Rican population according to elementary school enrollment from 1958 to 1966. The densest concentration of Puerto Ricans since 1950 has been in the

Fig. 5–2 Area of Puerto Rican Settlement in Brooklyn by Census Tracts, 1935. Reproduced from Lawrence R. Chenault, *The Puerto Rican Migrant in New York City* (New York: Columbia University Press, 1938), Fig. 3, p. 105, by permission of Columbia University Press.

South Bronx, but the East Harlem community continues to be the area most completely associated with the Puerto Rican community. Called "The Barrio" (The Puerto Rican Neighborhood), it is identified with Puerto Ricans in a way that no other area of the city has been.

The significant thing about the population has been its rapid spread. By 1966, according to the school maps, in every school district in Manhattan, in all but one in the Bronx, and in all but three in Brooklyn, Puerto Ricans constituted 12.5 per cent or more of the public school population. In 1958, only one district in the City, the South Bronx, had a school population more than 50 per cent Puerto Rican; in 1966, four districts had gone beyond 50 per cent Puerto Rican. They were South Bronx, South Central Bronx, Manhattan's Lower East Side, and the Williamsburg section of Brooklyn. Statistics do not tell the entire story, however. Puerto Ricans have been a very mobile population within the

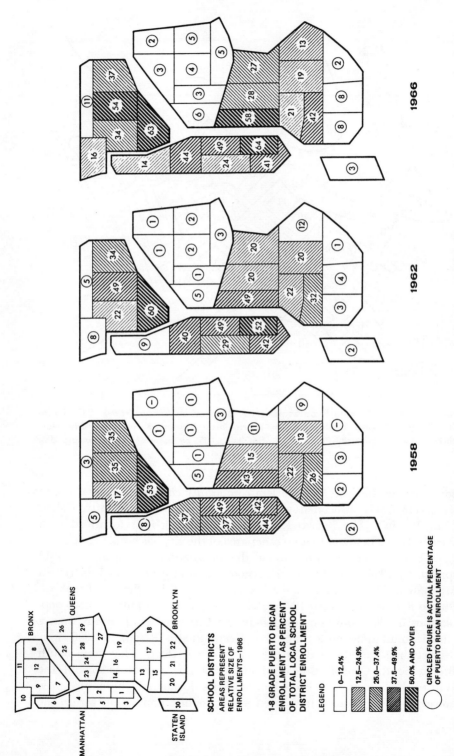

Fig. 5–3 Puerto Rican Student Enrollment in New York City, by Boroughs, 1958–1966. Reproduced from New York City Board of Education Special School Census, October 31, 1958, 1962, and 1966.

City because of large scale urban renewal projects, relocation due to housing developments, and a propensity to move quickly while looking for a little better place to live. In an unpublished study of a small section of the Lower East Side, Manhattan, carried out in 1958 by students of the Sociology Department of Fordham University, 28 Puerto Rican families were identified on one block in March 1958; there were still 28 Puerto Rican families on the block in November of the same year, but 21 of them were different families.

Although Puerto Ricans are scattered widely throughout the City, and are concentrated in some areas, it is doubtful whether they have established those geographical concentrations which were so important to the strong communities of earlier immigrant groups. One key to the strength of the earlier immigrants was the pattern of housing. At the point of second settlement, the earlier immigrants began to establish their tightly knit, strong communities. They could move into housing which was new, but within the rental range of poor working class families. This was private housing, and immigrants moved into the same house or block where brothers, cousins, aunts, relatives, or friends had moved before them. These dense concentrations gave rise to large areas which became the Little Dublins, or the Little Italies, the Little Germanies, the large concentrations of Jewish people, or others. They became stable, settled communities where a particular style of life was established and maintained. However, the only housing within reasonable range of the income of the Puerto Ricans is the public housing projects. Selection for these is on a nondiscriminatory basis according to policy norms of the New York City Housing Authority. Therefore, Puerto Ricans cannot easily move in where brothers, cousins, relatives, or friends are living, and find themselves within a conglomerate group. It is obviously much more difficult to maintain the cohesiveness of a stable Puerto Rican community similar to that of early immigrant groups.

Political Representation

One effect of this scattering of the Puerto Rican population is a weakening of its potential political strength. There are relatively few districts in which the Puerto Ricans alone could carry an election. Where they have a large percentage of the population, their voting power is affected by two other factors: a large percentage of the Puerto Rican population is still below voting age, and many of those who have reached voting age have not registered. Until 1964, Puerto Ricans in New York State were required to take a literacy test in English before they were permitted to register. This requirement was ruled out by the Civil Rights Act of 1965 and Puerto Ricans not literate in English may now register simply by showing evidence of having completed 6 years of schooling in Puerto Rico. The registration of Puerto Ricans which followed this change of the law was probably the reason for the election of Herman Badillo, a Puerto Rican, as Bronx Borough President in 1965. He won the election by a slim margin of about 2,000 votes, and probably would have lost without the support of newly registered Puerto Ricans. However, even with the new provisions for registration, Puerto Ricans have not been registering in large numbers. In the summer of 1969, a special drive was held to register Black and Puerto Rican voters. It fell far short of expectations. The Citizens Voter Registration Campaign estimated that 131,000 Puerto Ricans were registered in the City of New York out of a potential voting body of 435,000.[3]

When Puerto Ricans do register and vote, they vote predominantly Democratic. Hubert Humphrey received about 93 per cent of the Puerto Rican vote in the 1968 election. The tendency to vote Democratic, even against Puerto Rican candidates, was further evidenced in the 1968 elections. The vote in predominantly Puerto Rican East Harlem was 88 per cent for Hulan Jack, a Black candidate for the State Assembly on the Democratic ticket, against 14 per cent for a Puerto Rican on the Republican ticket. In the 1968 election for State Senator from the East Harlem–South Bronx District, three Puerto Ricans were running against each other. Roberto Garcia, the Democratic candidate, won 85 per cent of the votes.

The low percentages of Puerto Ricans in many districts, and their low percentage of registered voters, has left the Puerto Ricans with no elected representatives in the New York City Government as of 1970, and with only four elected representatives in the New York State Government, one State Senator, Roberto Garcia, and three Assemblymen, Armando Montano, Luis Nine, and Manuel Ramos. All three are from the South Bronx.[4] This weak position does not speak well for the political strength of the Puerto Rican community at the present moment. Strong political action both proceeds from community strength and contributes to an increase of community strength.

The most important political figure to appear in the Puerto Rican community thus far has been Herman Badillo Rivera. Born in 1929 in Caguas, a Puerto Rican city near San Juan, he came to the mainland after the death of his parents when he was 12 years old. He always calls attention to the fact that he put himself through school by working at three types of jobs, pin boy, elevator operator, and dishwasher, all of which

[3] *The New York Times*, August 26, 1969, p. 33.
[4] *The New York Times*, October 15, 1970, p. 30.

have since been eliminated by machines. He won his A.B. degree at City College and his law degree at Brooklyn Law School. He was one of a small group of bright, young Puerto Rican men and women who inaugurated a number of grass-roots movements in the 1950's to improve the life of Puerto Rican youth in the City of New York. He entered politics in 1961 and received his first important political appointment in 1962, when he was named Commissioner of the newly created Office of Relocation. When criticized for his handling of the relocation of many Puerto Rican families, he frequently told his audiences or his friends "I have been relocated so often in my life that I probably have a better understanding of relocation than most persons." He was elected Borough President of the Bronx in 1965; he resigned in the Spring of 1969 to run in the primary election for Democratic candidate for Mayor but was defeated. He ran in the 1970 election as the Democratic and Liberal Party candidate for the House of Representatives from the Hunts Point Section of the Bronx and was elected. He is the first elected Puerto Rican Congressman, and has also been named a Distinguished Professor of Urban Education by the Graduate School of Education of Fordham University in New York for the year 1970–1971. This is a record of success which matches the impressive rise to power of many of the best known political leaders of earlier immigrant groups. He is the outstanding political figure in the community. Antonio "Tony" Mendez has long been a figure in Democratic politics in East Harlem, and Mrs. Amalia Betanzos is active on the West Side. Mrs. Encarnacion Armas has been active in the Liberal Party but, despite her efforts, the Liberal Party has never been able to build a constituency among the Puerto Ricans of the City. Thus it is the younger people such as Badillo and Roberto Garcia who are giving the political character to the population at the present time.

Education and Occupational Levels

Occupationally and educationally, the Puerto Ricans are the poorest segment of the New York City population. In comparison with Blacks and the non-Puerto Rican population, they are heavily concentrated in the low occupational levels, and their median family income is considerably lower than that of the Blacks. The *Profile of the Bronx Economy*,[5] completed in 1967, indicated that median family income of Puerto Rican families in the Bronx was $400 lower than that of the Blacks. Table 5–1 presents the data on family income for the City of New York based on 1960 census reports. At that time, 53.7 per cent of the Puerto Rican fami-

[5] *A Profile of the Bronx Economy*, Institute for Urban Studies, Fordham University, Bronx, New York, 1967, mimeo'd.

TABLE 5–1

FAMILY INCOME BY ETHNIC GROUP,
NEW YORK CITY, 1960

	Percentages of Families with Income[a]		
Income	Puerto Rican	Nonwhite	Other White
Under $3,000	33.8	27.1	11.8
Under $4,000	53.7	43.6	19.2
$4,000 and over	46.3	56.4	80.8

SOURCE: U.S. Bureau of the Census. *U.S. Census of Population and Housing, 1960.* Census Tracts. Final Report PHC (1)-104. Part 1 (Washington, D.C.: U.S. Government Printing Office, 1962). Tables P-1, P-4, P-5.

[a]Nonadditive. Families with less than $4,000 income includes those with less than $3,000 income.

lies had family incomes below the $4,000 mark, whereas only 43.6 per cent of the nonwhite families were below that level. The *Profile of the Bronx Economy* also indicated that high rates of unemployment were found in the same areas where levels of education were low. Most of the Puerto Ricans covered by the study in the *Profile* had been born on the Island and migrated to the mainland. Of Puerto Ricans coming to the mainland between 1957 and 1961, 45 per cent were between 15–24 years of age; 53 per cent of all migrants had had no previous work experience.

Table 5–2 presents the occupational levels of the Puerto Rican population in New York City according to the 1960 census. In both 1950 and 1960 Puerto Ricans were concentrated in the operative and nonhousehold service categories. These are predominantly unskilled and semiskilled occupations. It is important, however, to note the difference between the first generation and the second, because an impressive improvement is indicated in the occupational levels of second generation Puerto Ricans. The only difficulty with this evidence for 1950 and 1960 is the fact that relatively few second generation Puerto Ricans were in the labor force in those years. At the time of the 1970 census, many more second generation Puerto Ricans had entered the labor force, so the results of that census will be significant in indicating whether the impressive progress of 1950 and 1960 continued during the following decade.

Statistics fail to reflect the impact of Puerto Ricans on the New York City job market. They dominate the hotel and restaurant trades to such an extent that these businesses would now be helpless without them. Puerto Rican women particularly constitute a significant part of the labor

TABLE 5–2

OCCUPATIONAL STATUS OF PERSONS BORN IN PUERTO RICO
AND OF PUERTO RICAN PARENTAGE, BY SEX,
NEW YORK CITY, 1950 AND 1960

Occupation	Born in Puerto Rico		Puerto Rican Parents	
	1950	1960	1950	1960
Males employed and occupation reported	46,275	118,288	3,585	9,096
Per cent	100.0	100.0	100.0	100.0
Professional technicians and kindred workers	2.4	1.8	5.4	7.4
Office managers and proprietors	5.5	3.7	4.4	4.0
Clerical, sales, and kindred workers	9.2	11.4	20.5	23.8
Craftsmen, foremen, and kindred workers	11.0	10.8	11.9	16.3
Operatives and kindred workers	37.4	45.2	35.4	29.8
Nonhousehold service workers	29.3	21.1	16.3	12.5
Household service	0.1	0.1	0.0	0.2
Laborers except farm and mine	5.0	5.7	6.0	6.0
Farm laborers and foremen	0.1	0.3	0.0	0.0
Females employed and occupation reported	31,730	61,225	2,955	5,893
Per cent	100.0	100.0	100.0	100.0
Professional technicians and kindred workers	1.7	2.6	5.6	6.3
Office managers and proprietors	1.0	1.1	1.2	1.7
Clerical, sales, and kindred workers	6.4	12.1	39.4	56.0
Craftsmen, foremen, and kindred workers	1.7	1.9	2.0	1.7
Operatives and kindred workers	80.8	74.0	40.9	24.4
Nonhousehold service workers	5.7	6.7	8.6	8.7
Household service	1.6	0.8	1.7	0.5
Laborers except farm and mine	1.0	0.8	0.5	0.6
Farm laborers and foremen	0.0	0.0	0.0	0.0

SOURCE: U.S. Bureau of the Census, *U.S. Census of Population, 1960. Subject Reports. Puerto Ricans in the United States.* Final Report. PC(2)-1D. (Washington, D.C.: U.S. Government Printing Office, 1963), Table 11.

force in the garment industry, which has always been the colorful and often turbulent source of employment for newcomers to the City. Irish and German tailors dominated the garment industry in the midnineteenth century. They were followed by the Jews and Italians, and now Blacks and Puerto Ricans constitute a large part of this labor force. The International Ladies Garment Workers Union, which has always been synonymous with immigrant efforts toward economic security, boasts that it is now the organization of the Black and Puerto Rican workers. However, Puerto Ricans have frequently complained that top union positions are still in the hands of an establishment from previous generations and of immigrant groups who prevent the advance of the Puerto Ricans to positions of union leadership and power. Unskilled and semiskilled factory work accounts for the employment of large numbers of Puerto Rican men and women, as reflected in the operative category of the census reports. The occupational advance from first to second generation is generally a move into the ranks of craftsmen and skilled workers for the men, and into the ranks of white collar clerical and sales employees for both men and women. At the same time, the increase in the percentage of second generation Puerto Rican men in professional and technical work is impressive.

Organizations of the
Puerto Rican Community

It is difficult to present a clear picture of the way the Puerto Rican community is structured, how it operates, and what gives it its community character. It is a highly dispersed community with a very large percentage of poor people, and it has not yet reached the level of sophistication in organizational activity which is evident in older, more established groups. Furthermore, the Puerto Rican community has been troubled by internal divisions and controversies.

In order to form some general outline of the way the Puerto Rican community functions, it seems best to give a brief description of a number of organizations which have played a significant role in its history in New York, and to indicate the particular significance of each of these organizations.

Two of the oldest Puerto Rican organizations in the city are the Puerto Rican Merchants Association and the Puerto Rican Civil Service Employees Association. The history of small business among Puerto Ricans is a colorful reflection of migrant experience in New York City. The small *Bodegas* or *Colmados* (grocery stores) dot every Puerto Rican neighborhood, as do the small cafes, bars, restaurants, and *botanicas*, which sell medicinal herbs, materials for spiritist activities, charms, religious goods, and a host of related objects. Travel agencies are numerous, with their attractive advertisements for travel back and forth to the Island: *Vuele ahora y paga despues* ("Fly now; pay later") brings a Puerto Rican to the Island for a few dollars down and small payments per month. The Puerto Rican Merchants Association has been an important economic network for the Puerto Rican community, although it has not been as politically or socially dynamic as the community organizations which will be mentioned later. Nevertheless, it has been a significant factor in assisting Puerto Ricans to advance into small private business.

The history of one of the founders of the Puerto Rican Merchants Association, Julio Hernandez, reflects the experience of upwardly mobile Puerto Ricans. Julio came from a family of eight children. His father had been well educated in Puerto Rico—eight years of schooling—had had a "good job" in Puerto Rico, and had been very interested in politics. In the late 1920's the family relocated to New York, where Julio was born shortly after. Caught in the depression, the family suffered from poverty in the early 1930's, but each of the children was educated at least to the end of high school. Julio Hernandez went on to Maritime Training School and served as an officer in the Merchant Marine for ten years. After his marriage he settled in Brooklyn, opened a grocery store, and then a restaurant. Out of these activities he moved toward the establishment of the Puerto Rican Merchants Association, and served as its Executive Secretary for several years. He became increasingly active in the Puerto Rican community, and during the 1960's became the director of several government programs to promote small business among Puerto Ricans in the city. He now serves on a wide range of boards of community centers, health associations, and civic and charitable organizations. He represents the Puerto Rican entrepreneur, as well as the merchant who seeks to relate himself to the service of a struggling community of newcomers to the City of New York.

Office of the Commonwealth of Puerto Rico. In 1948, when the post-World War II migration from Puerto Rico was beginning to increase, Governor Muñoz Marin established an office in New York, supported by the Government of Puerto Rico, to assist the increasing numbers of Puerto Ricans coming to the city. The office was created to fulfill a number of functions: (1) to supervise the program of contract farm workers who were brought to the mainland to work on farms, and were expected to return to Puerto Rico at the end of the three, four, six month, or other contract period; (2) to provide an employment service to assist Puerto Ricans in getting jobs; (3) to identify Puerto Ricans as Puerto Ricans;[6] (4) to provide a social service referral program to direct Puerto Ricans to a variety of social service resources which could help them; (5) to provide a function of educational counseling, involving location of financial assistance for promising Puerto Rican students, and provision of educational guidance for them; (6) to provide a variety of services

[6]Apparently many Spanish-speaking persons who are not citizens of the United States present themselves as Puerto Ricans in order to enjoy the privileges of citizenship. They are often challenged when they do so. In the process, however, many Puerto Ricans are also challenged, and they must establish their identity as Puerto Ricans. The Office of the Commonwealth undertook this function.

to the Puerto Rican community which can be defined as aspects of a community organization function, in other words, to assist the local Puerto Rican communities throughout the city to identify and exploit their resources for their own advancement and development. The Office was to fulfill another related function. As a public relations instrument, it has provided information about Puerto Rico and Puerto Ricans to New Yorkers, and information about New York to Puerto Ricans.

In many ways the Office of the Commonwealth found itself representing the New York Puerto Ricans. Its officials and employees were regularly called upon by public and private agencies to present "the Puerto Rican point of view." It provided testimony at public hearings in which Puerto Rico or Puerto Ricans had an interest. On many occasions it sought either formally or informally to coordinate the activities of other Puerto Rican organizations in the City. The Office has been a tangible point to which people turn when they wish to contact the Puerto Rican community. It has given visibility in an organized way to the Puerto Ricans of New York.

It has not been without its controversial aspects, however. Not only is it a government office, it is an office of the Government in Puerto Rico. This has involved a number of unfavorable consequences. New York Puerto Ricans who wish to manage their own lives and have confidence in their ability to do their own thing resent its presence in New York. They have been critical of a situation in which they, as New Yorkers, seemed to be represented by an arm of the Government of Puerto Rico. This has become more acute as the number of New York born Puerto Ricans has increased. Furthermore, as a government office, the Office of the Commonwealth has never been able to transcend political identification. During the regime of the Popular Party in Puerto Rico, the Office was staffed by people who shared their political position; with the election of Luis Ferre by the New Party, a director has been appointed who endorses his political ideas and goals. As a result, there has always been some ambiguity about the response of the Office to the political realities of Puerto Ricans in New York. During the 1960's, the Office of the Commonwealth was directed by Joseph Monserrat. He was born in Puerto Rico, came to New York as a small child and was raised there, so he identifies himself more a second generation than a first generation Puerto Rican. As Director of the Office he became a significant but continually controversial influence in the Puerto Rican community. He has been an articulate and intelligent spokesman for the community on many occasions, but his role was always complicated by the political character of the position he held. When he resigned from the Office in 1969, he was appointed to the interim Board of Education by then Bronx Borough President

Badillo; he was elected President of the Interim Board by its membership and distinguished himself at a moment of critical tension and transition for the educational system of New York City. Mr. Manuel Cassiano, appointed director in 1969, was born in the South Bronx and raised himself from poverty to become a skillful and wealthy business man. He represents that small segment of second generation Puerto Ricans who have advanced dramatically during the past 20 years. He now shifts into the area of community service, and brings to the task the expertise of the successful business executive. In late 1970, Cassiano was named Director of the Puerto Rico Industrial Development Company, a public corporation with responsibility for promoting the industrial development on the Island. Its activities are popularly known as "Operation Bootstrap." This is an interesting reversal, the appointment of a New Yorker to a position in San Juan. No one has yet been named successor to Cassiano as Director of the Office of the Commonwealth.

At the time of this writing, in the Fall of 1970, the Office was in a state of transition. Other grass-roots New York Puerto Rican organizations have emerged which deal with problems of education, social service, employment, and community organization, thus raising the question as to whether the Office of the Commonwealth should continue these services. The present thrust of the Office is in the direction of job development and training.

In view of the continuing migration of poor Puerto Ricans to New York, the Office may still have an important function to fulfill in helping them in their adjustment to the city. It is doubtful whether it will have much influence among young New York born Puerto Ricans who are moving into adulthood. Some militant young Puerto Ricans recently picketed the Office, protesting the role of the Office in the contract farm workers program. The young people claimed that Puerto Rican farm workers who were working under contract on farms of the mainland were being exploited and treated unjustly. They demanded that the Office terminate the program. The future of the Office therefore cannot be clearly seen at the present moment. It may continue to fulfill some important services but it is doubtful that it will be as significant an organization in the future of the New York Puerto Rican community as it has been in the past.

The Puerto Rican Forum. In the mid-1950's, a group of young, intelligent Puerto Ricans saw the need of a communitywide organization to promote the interests of Puerto Ricans in New York City, and so they established the Puerto Rican Forum. These young, vigorous, interested people of the early 1950's have since come to distinguish themselves for their service to the Puerto Rican Community.

They were primarily concerned with the development of Puerto
Rican youth, and their efforts were in the direction of educational
achievement. However, they were aware of the need for a range of other
programs for the strengthening of the Puerto Rican community in New
York City. Two major developments resulted from their efforts: the founding of Aspira, an organization to promote education among Puerto
Ricans, and the Puerto Rican Community Development Project, a city-
wide agency to promote programs of many kinds in local Puerto Rican
communities.

The Forum remains a central and significant organization of Puerto
Ricans. It probably comes closest to being a representative organization
of Puerto Ricans in New York. It promotes programs which it carries out
itself; it promotes programs and funding for programs which are carried
out by local Puerto Rican organizations; it is generally represented at
meetings or on committees where a Puerto Rican voice is expected to be
heard. It is a highly respected and influential voice for the Puerto Rican
community.

Aspira. One of the early organizations founded by the Puerto Rican
Forum was an agency to promote higher education for Puerto Ricans.
It was given the Spanish name of *Aspira*, which means *strive* or *aspire*.
Founded in 1961 to provide inspiration and guidance to Puerto Rican
youths to continue their education into the professions, technical fields,
and the arts, Aspira has sought to identify promising Puerto Rican youths,
to motivate them to continue their education, to provide educational
guidance and leadership, and to promote scholarships and financial aid
to assist them in financing their education. Aspira has also been devoted
to the development of a sense of self-confidence and identity among
Puerto Rican youth by familiarizing them with their own cultural background and the cultural achievements of the Island.

Of all the grass-roots organizations of the Puerto Rican community,
Aspira has probably been the most effective. It has become nationally
known, and its service to Puerto Rican youth has been remarkable. Many
of the young people now coming out of colleges and professional schools
received their early encouragement and guidance from Aspira. The Aspira
staff has spoken for the Puerto Rican community on educational issues,
and has had considerable influence in the development of programs promoting Puerto Rican education. They have established Aspira clubs in
many of the high schools throughout the city, and have conducted workshops and conferences for both educators and youth. The Conference
on Puerto Rican Education which Aspira conducted in 1968 received
nationwide attention.

The inspiration and guiding spirit of Aspira was Antonia Pantoja, a Puerto Rican woman born on the Island, raised and educated in New York, and with a professional degree as a social worker. She was active with Puerto Rican youth groups in the early 1950's, and was one of the founders of the Puerto Rican Forum. She spent a number of years on the Mayor's Committee on Human Rights, and later began to devote almost all of her time to Aspira. In 1968 she returned to Puerto Rico, where she developed Aspira Clubs and acted as a consultant on private and public projects. In 1971 she returned to Washington, D.C. as a consultant. She has been one of the significant persons in the Puerto Rican community during the past decade.

Aspira represents an orientation toward education, professional training, and competence as the means of advancing in American society. It has not been without its critics. Another segment of the Puerto Rican community moved toward more direct forms of community and political action, leading to the founding of the Puerto Rican Community Development Project. There has been tension between the representatives of these two different orientations, the one intellectual and stressing the need for professional achievement, the other urging direct community action.

Criticism has also developed from among the militant student groups in the city. They tend to identify Aspira with the Establishment and reject an association with it in favor of action aimed at more radical educational reforms. But in terms of solid and tangible achievement, probably no other Puerto Rican organization can show as much evidence of accomplishment as Aspira.

Puerto Rican Community Development Project. Shortly after the founding of Aspira, members of the Forum saw the need for a more comprehensive development program for the Puerto Rican community. The leading figure in this movement was also Antonia Pantoja. The interested Puerto Ricans pursued a program which would promote a sense of identity among Puerto Ricans in New York, and would help them develop community strength. This was based on the sociological position (indicated in Chapter Three) that newcomers integrate from a position of strength, and that it was the strong, stable immigrant communities which enabled earlier immigrants to move steadily and confidently into the mainstream of American society.

This theory was elaborated in an excellent position paper prepared by Professor Frank Bonilla, then of the faculty of M.I.T., and a project was proposed which would provide a range of services to the Puerto Rican community aimed at promoting identity, community stability, and political strength. The Bonilla paper is a significant document in the literature on cultural assimilation, and the final proposal for the Puerto Rican Community Development Project[7] remains an impressive description of the Puerto Rican community in New York City as of 1964.

Two unfortunate things happened in the development of the proposal. First, the Puerto Ricans promoting the project split into two factions over the promotion of the proposal and the anticipated control of the project. The separation reflected the two orientations indicated above. One group represented the views of those Puerto Ricans who thought in terms of long range educational and professional advancement, and the development of high level competence among young Puerto Ricans. The other orientation looked to more immediate community action, and sought to mobilize community pressure for prompt improvement of conditions among Puerto Ricans. Second, the City of New York refused to fund the project while it was under the control of those with the long range orientation. City officials argued that: (1) they could not fund a project identified with one ethnic group (even though the Puerto Ricans agreed to provide services on a nondiscriminatory basis to all ethnic and racial groups of the city); (2) the project, which was intended as citywide, would duplicate services already provided by community corporations; and (3) the philosophy of the project, aimed at identity and strength for the Puerto Rican community, was much too vague. The city wanted to fund projects more on the "nuts and bolts" level of jobs and immediate income. The refusal to fund the project aggravated the split among the Forum members. The community action proponents were able to take over the proposal, and eventually succeeded in getting it funded. They have been the significant figures in it ever since.

The Puerto Rican Community Development Project was first funded in 1965 by the Office of Economic Opportunity. It is citywide, and, in turn, funds a large number of projects throughout the city. It has become involved in job training programs, tutoring programs, neighborhood youth corps, addiction prevention programs, and a block program of community organization. Even more important than these programs, however, has been the Project's role as a visible representative of Puerto Ricans in New York. The Project has been troubled by internal struggles for control, but it has succeeded in giving politically militant voice to the Puerto Rican community when Puerto Rican interests have been at stake. It has mounted demonstrations before City Hall and before numerous city agencies to protest mistreatment of Puerto Ricans or to demand

---

[7]Puerto Rican Forum, Inc., *The Puerto Rican Community Development Project: A Proposal for a Self-help Project to Develop the Community by Strengthening the Family, Opening Opportunities for Youth, and Making Full Use of Education.* Unpublished proposal, New York, 1963.

Puerto Rican rights. It is regrettable that much of this activity has been directed at Black citizens, with the charge that Blacks have gained strategic control over the poverty program. This controversy became intense in the Autumn of 1970 when an effort was made by the Community Development Agency of the Human Resources Administration of New York City to terminate the funding provided by the antipoverty program to citywide agencies.[8] Three of the most important citywide agencies are Puerto Rican: Aspira, The Puerto Rican Family Institute, and the Puerto Rican Community Development Project. The Director of the Community Development Agency happened to be Black, and the animosity of the Puerto Rican community was directed toward him in what appeared to be a Black vs. Puerto Rican conflict of interests over the control of antipoverty funds.[9]

If the funds from the antipoverty program are withdrawn, the Puerto Rican Community Development Project hopes to continue to operate with funds from a variety of other sources. It is one of the few citywide projects which serve Puerto Ricans and represent them in a militant style when the occasion arises.

The Puerto Rican Family Institute. The Puerto Rican Family Institute represents the grass-roots Puerto Rican effort in the area of professional social service. It was established as a voluntary agency in 1963 by a small group of Puerto Rican social workers led by Augustino Gonzales, assisted by a team of volunteers who were affectionately called, in Puerto Rican style, "Godparents." The objective of the agency was to create for newly arrived Puerto Rican families the support of an extended ritual kinship system which is a major feature of the culture of the Island. They sought to identify Puerto Rican families which had established themselves on the mainland, and, with their help, to enable newly arrived families to cope with the problems of establishing themselves firmly in New York City. The Family Institute was given support by the Council against Poverty as a citywide agency in 1965; with the help of antipoverty funds, it has been serving the Puerto Rican community ever since. It has extended its staff and, together with its program of attempting to match integrated families with those newly arrived, provides a range of direct

[8]The Community Development Agency claimed, among other things, that the antipoverty funds should be disbursed through the local community corporations in the poverty areas, and that the citywide agencies were not properly related to these local corporations. Community corporations are the local agencies established in sections of the city which are defined as "poverty areas," and administer the funds assigned to that area for local antipoverty programs. The governing boards of community corporations are elected by the people of the area.

[9]*The New York Times*, September 4, 1970, p. 24; September 7, 1970, p. 22; September 11, 1970, p. 83. See also notes 15 and 16 in Chapter Seven.

services to prevent family disruption through family case work, psychiatric and social work counseling.

The Puerto Rican Family Institute is the only grass-roots Puerto Rican family agency in New York City. Staffed by Puerto Ricans and conducted in a thoroughly Puerto Rican style, it provides a setting where Puerto Rican families feel at home and can seek assistance which is provided without the strangeness and unfamiliar complications of a professional New York agency. It has been criticized for its conventional, case work orientation. But, in terms of direct social service, it is a Puerto Rican oasis in a desert of bewildering agencies, and hundreds of Puerto Rican families seek it out as a refuge in a strange land.

These agencies, the Office of the Commonwealth, the Forum, Aspira, the Community Development Project, and the Family Institute represent, to a large extent, the organized face of the Puerto Rican community on a citywide basis.

There is a range of other organizations, including the clubs involving New York residents from practically every small town in Puerto Rico, which are centers of social activity, mutual help, and friendly support. There are active athletic leagues, and cultural organizations such as the Instituto de Puerto Rico and the Ateneo de Puerto Rico which are dedicated to cultivating literature, music, and the arts among New York Puerto Ricans. New theatre groups are beginning to appear, such as the eminently successful Puerto Rican Traveling Theatre, founded by Miriam Colon, which tours the streets in summertime presenting Puerto Rican dramas to the people of the neighborhoods. There are action groups, such as United Bronx Parents, which carries on a vigorous campaign for improvement of the schools in the poor sections of the Bronx. It was founded and continues under the militant guidance of a Puerto Rican woman, Evelina Antonetti. Although many of its participants are Puerto Rican, it provides a service to the entire neighborhood with regard to conditions in the schools.

What is the Puerto Rican community in New York? Is it an entity? How does it function? Does it have an identity, a visibility, the quality of a clearly recognizable segment of the city? Containing probably a million people in 1970, it constitutes the largest Puerto Rican city in the world, about one-third larger than the city of San Juan; its population is about 40 per cent of the size of the entire population of Puerto Rico. It is a population mainly of poor working people, the backbone of the labor force for hotels, restaurants, hospitals, the garment industry, small factories, and shops, without whom the economy of the city would collapse. It is youthful, now about one-fourth of the entire public school population of the city. Puerto Ricans constitute one-half of the membership of the entire New York Archdiocese, but there are only six Puerto Rican priests in the city. There is a small but steadily growing number of Puerto Rican policemen and firemen. There are five Puerto Rican school principals in the city, and a small percentage of Puerto Rican teachers. About 25 per cent of the eligible Puerto Rican voters are registered, and not a single Puerto Rican holds an elected office in New York City. There are three City Commissioners who are Puerto Rican (Marta Valle, Commissioner of the Youth Services Agency, Amalia Bentanzos, Commissioner of Relocation and Joseph Rodriquez Erazo, Commissioner of the Manpower and Career Development Agency), and some Deputy Commissioners in the Human Resources Administration and in the Housing Authority and Police Department. A large number of small businesses are represented in the Puerto Rican Merchants Association; a small number of professionals, social workers, doctors, and lawyers are beginning to take an active and militant role in support of their people. There are a few community corporations in which Puerto Ricans have an influential or dominant voice in East Harlem and the Lower East Side in Manhattan, Coney Island and Williamsburg in Brooklyn, and South Bronx, Hunts Point, and Tremont in the Bronx. There is one newspaper, *El Diario de Nueva York,* owned by a mainland American and staffed by Puerto Ricans, which is known as the Puerto Rican paper. Although they are only about 15 per cent of the city's population, Puerto Ricans constitute about 40 per cent of the recipients of public welfare in the form of Aid to Dependent Children; about 23 per cent of the registered heroin addicts are Puerto Rican.

All this adds up to a struggling, suffering, poor, but vital segment of the city. It is a community without a visible, powerful leader, and one which has not been able to make a unified impact on the city proportionate to its representation in the population. The community is continually losing experienced persons to the Island in return migration, and is replenishing its poorest ranks with newcomers from the Island. It stands at an uncertain moment in its struggle for stability, identity, and strength.

The second generation increases, but its future is still unknown. Available data reveal an impressive advance, socially and economically, of the second generation. A new style is appearing among the youth. The larger numbers entering college are militant and aggressive. They took a leading part in the demonstrations which shut down City College in the Spring of 1969, and in the militant action at Queens, Brooklyn, and Lehman Colleges which resulted in the establishment of Puerto Rican studies programs. Since 1968 the Young Lords have appeared as a demonstrative group of militant Puerto Ricans. They occupied a church in East Harlem in the Spring of 1970, engaged in militant action around Metropolitan and Gouverneur Hospitals, and were involved in aggressive demonstrations around Lincoln Hospital in the Bronx in the Autumn of

1970. As will be indicated later, although they constitute a controversial development within the Puerto Rican community, they are a clear sign that the second generation Puerto Ricans are likely to be different from the first.

PUERTO RICANS ON THE MAINLAND:

The Educational Experience *

The Migration and Mainland Experience: An Overview

In February 1971, the U.S. Census Bureau published its November 1969, sample-survey estimate that the fifty states and the District of Columbia had 1,454,000 Puerto Rican residents—811,000 born on the island, 636,000 born in the states and district, 1,000 in Cuba, and 6,000 elsewhere. In March 1972, the Census Bureau released preliminary and a few final state population totals from the 1970 census for three categories—persons of Spanish language, persons of Spanish family name, and Puerto Ricans. Puerto Rican counts were for three states only—New York (872,471; 5% of the state population); New Jersey (135,676; 2% of the state population); and Pennsylvania (44,535).

Puerto Ricans have been on the mainland for many years; in the 19th century, a small colony of Puerto Ricans, gathered largely in New York City, worked for the independence of the island. After the annexation of the island in 1898 by the United States, a continuing migration to the mainland began. In 1910 some 1,500 Puerto Ricans were living in the United States; by 1930, they numbered close to 53,000. The migration was reversed during the depression of the 1930s; and again was substantially impeded by World War II in the early 1940s. After the end of World War II (and concurrent with the advent of cheap air transport) it increased steadily until it reached its peak in the early 1950s (in 1953, *304,910* persons left the island and *203,307* returned, leaving a net balance of *74,603*). The state of the economy on the mainland has always been an indicator of the migration. The decline in Puerto Rican migration to the mainland in 1970 and continuing into 1971 was precisely due to economic hardship in the states.[1]

In a prescient book on Puerto Rican Americans, the Jesuit sociologist, Rev. Joseph P. Fitzpatrick, observes that Puerto Ricans have found it difficult to achieve "community solidarity" and suggests that they may work out adjustment "in very new ways" differing from those of past immigrants (technically, as American citizens, Puerto Ricans are migrants to the mainland United States); and Father Fitzpatrick cogently observes:

[1] For Puerto Rico passenger traffic for fiscal years 1940–1969, see the reports of the Puerto Rico Planning Board. The major source of information on Puerto Rican migration is the Department of Labor, Migration Division, Commonwealth of Puerto Rico. See further H. C. Barton, Jr., "The Employment Situation in Puerto Rico and Migratory Movements between Puerto Rico and the United States," *Summary of Proceedings: Workshop on Employment Problems of Puerto Ricans* (Graduate School of Social Work, New York University, 1968). See also *The New York Puerto Rican: Patterns of Work Experience.* U.S. Department of Labor. Bureau of Labor Statistics [Middle Atlantic Regional Office], New York, 1971.

* Francesco Cordasco, "Puerto Ricans on the Mainland: The Educational Experience," The Puerto Rican Study, 1953-1957: A Report on the Education and Adjustment of Puerto Rican Pupils in the Public Schools of the City of New York (New York: Oriole Editions, 1972), pp. iii-xxiii.

A book about the Puerto Ricans in mainland United States, with a special focus on those in New York City, is very risky but also is very necessary. It is risky because the Puerto Rican community is in a state of turbulent change in a city and a nation which are also in a state of turbulent change. So many different currents of change affect Puerto Ricans at the present time that it is foolhardy to attempt to describe this group adequately or put them into focus. Nor is it possible to point out clearly any one direction in which the Puerto Rican community is moving in its adjustment to life on the mainland. Its directions are often in conflict, and no single leader or movement has given sharp definition to one direction as dominant over others. . . . What is most needed at this moment of the Puerto Rican experience, both for Puerto Ricans and other mainland Americans, is *perspective:* a sense of the meaning of the migration for everyone involved in that migration, for the new-comers as well as the residents of the cities and neighborhoods to which the Puerto Ricans come.[2]

How varied the Puerto Rican experience on the mainland has been can be best indicated by the sharp contrasts provided in four juxtaposed excerpts from Puerto Rican reactions registered over a period of time.

In 1948, J. J. Osuna, the distinguished Puerto Rican educator, on a visit to New York City schools, observed:

As far as possible something should be done in Puerto Rico to discourage migration of people who do not have occupations to go into upon their arrival in this country, or of children whose parents live in Puerto Rico and who have no home in New York. Too many people are coming, hoping that they may find work and thereby better themselves economically, and in the case of the children, educationally. It is laudable that they take the chance, but the experience of the past teaches us that as far as possible, people should not come to the continent until they have secured employment here.[3]

In 1961, Joseph Monserrat, at the time Director of the Migration Division, Commonwealth of Puerto Rico, in speaking on "Community Planning for Puerto Rican Integration in the United States," cautioned that:

[2] Joseph P. Fitzpatrick, *Puerto Rican Americans: The Meaning of Migration to the Mainland* (Englewood Cliffs, N.J.: Prentice-Hall, 1971), p. xi. The Puerto Rican migration is, in many ways, a unique phenomenon for the United States. "The Puerto Ricans have come for the most part in the first great airborne migration of people from abroad; they are decidedly newcomers of the aviation age. A Puerto Rican can travel from San Juan to New Yok in less time than a New Yorker could travel from Coney Island to Times Square a century ago. They are the first group to come in large numbers from a different cultural background but who are, nevertheless, citizens of the United States. They are the first group of newcomers who bring a cultural practice of widespread intermingling and intermarriage of people of many different colors. They are the first group of predominantly Catholic migrants not accompanied by a native clergy. Numerous characteristics of the Puerto Ricans make their migration unique." (Fitzpatrick, p. 2)

[3] J. J. Osuna, *Report on Visits to New York City Schools* [Government of Puerto Rico]. Reprinted in F. Cordasco and E. Bucchioni, *Puerto Rican Children in Mainland Schools: A Sourcebook for Teachers* (Metuchen, N.J.: Scarecrow Press, 1968), pp. 227–239.

If all Puerto Ricans were to suddenly disappear from New York City, neither the housing problem nor other basic issues confronting the city would be solved. In fact, without the Puerto Ricans, New York would be faced with one of two alternatives: either "import" people to do the work done by Puerto Ricans (and whoever was imported from wherever they might come would have to live in the very same buildings Puerto Ricans now live in for the simple reason that there is nothing else); or industries would have to move to other areas where there are workers, causing a severe economic upheaval in the city. Obviously, neither one is a viable solution. Nor will the stagnation of the past resolve our dilemma. . . . The Puerto Rican, although he comes from a close knit neighborhood in the Commonwealth, has found the best possibility for social action and self-improvement on the city-wide level. The community of Puerto Ricans is not the East Side or the South Side. It is New York City, Lorain, Chicago, Los Angeles, Middletown. City living is learned living. The migrants must be helped to learn the facts of city life and how to function effectively as a pressure group in a pressure group society.[4]

Both of these statements are in stark contrast to the ideology of revolution and separatism evident in the animadversions which follow. First, from a spokesman for "La Generación Encojonada":

Violence is the essence of a colonial society. It is established as a system in the interests of the ruling classes. Colonial society "is the meeting of two forces, opposed to each other by their very nature, which in fact owe their originality to that sort of substantification which results from and is nourished by the situation in the colonies. Their first encounter was marked by violence and their existence together . . . was carried on by dint of a great array of bayonets and cannon." Puerto Rican history has been witness to this violent confrontation between people and oppressor. We see it in daily events: in schools, churches, factories, the countryside, in strikes, demonstrations, and insurrections. As soon as an individual confronts the system, he feels its violence in the way of life colonialism imposes on him: the feudal-type exploitation in the countryside, the capitalist exploitation in the cities.

The lifeblood of every colonial society is the profit it offers to its exploiters. Its basis is the authority of an exploiting system—not the authority that comes from a majority consensus, but the paternal authority with which a minority tries to justify a system beneficial to it. Around that system is built a morality, an ethic, rooted in the economic co-existence of colonizers and colonized. Thus the system envelops itself in forms that create the illusion of sharing, of a brotherhood and equality that don't exist. The Puerto Rican elections held every four years exemplify this.

[4] Joseph Monserrat, "Community Planning for Puerto Rican Integration in the United States" [An Address at the National Conference on Social Welfare, Minneapolis, Minnesota, May 1961]. Published in F. Cordasco and E. Bucchioni, *op. cit.*, pp. 221–226. ,

We must not confuse the ox with the fighting bull, the causes with the problem, the root with the branches.[5]

And from a theoretician for the Young Lords Party, spawned in the socio-pathology of the urban *barrio:*

> To support its economic exploitation of Puerto Rico, the United States instituted a new educational system whose purpose was to Americanize us. Specifically, that means that the school's principal job is to exalt the cultural values of the United States. As soon as we begin using books that are printed in English, that are printed in the United States, that means that the American way of life is being pushed . . . with all its bad points, with its commercialism, its dehumanization of human beings.
> At the same time that the cultural values of America are exalted, the cultural values of Puerto Rico are downgraded. People begin to feel ashamed of speaking Spanish. Language becomes a reward and punishment system. If you speak English and adapt to the cultural values of America, you're rewarded; if you speak Spanish and stick to the old traditional ways, you're punished. In the school system here, if you don't quickly begin to speak English and shed your Puerto Rican values, you're put back a grade —so you may be in the sixth grade in Puerto Rico but when you come here, you go back to the fourth or fifth. You're treated as if you're retarded, as if you're backward—and your own cultural values therefore are shown to be of less value than the cultural values of this country and the language of this country.[6]

It is no accident that this strident voice registers anger particularly with the schools; for, it is in the schools that Puerto Rican identity is subjected to the greatest pressures, and it is the educational experience on the mainland which, for Puerto Ricans, is generally bad and from which despair and alienation emerge. It is in mainland schools that the dynamics of conflict and acculturation for Puerto Ricans are best seen in clear perspective; and it is a grim irony that, generally, educational programs for Puerto Ricans have failed despite the multitudinous educational experiments encapsulated in those new attentions born in Johnsonian America to the culture of the poor and the massive programmatic onslaughts on

[5] Juan A. Silén, *We, The Puerto Rican People: A Story of Oppression and Resistance* (New York: Monthly Review Press, 1971), pp. 118–119. Originally, *Hacia una Visión Positiva del Puertorriqueño* (Rio Piedras: Editorial Edil, 1970).

[6] David Perez, "The Chains that have been Taken off Slaves' Bodies are put Back on their Minds." *Palante: Young Lords Party.* [Photographs by Michael Abramson; text by Young Lords Party and Michael Abramson.] (New York: McGraw-Hill, 1971), pp. 65–66. Palante is the Spanish equivalent of "Right On" or "Forward." The Young Lords Party is a revolutionary political organization formed in New York City in 1969. The concerns of the Young Lords Party range from prisons and health care to sexism; they have cleaned up the streets of *El Barrio,* organized free breakfast programs for school children, and conducted door-to-door testing for lead poisoning and tuberculosis. See Frank Browning, "From Rumble to Revolution: The Young Lords," *Ramparts* (October 1970); and Richard C. Schroeder, *Spanish-Americans: The New Militants.* Washington: Editorial Research Reports, 1971.

poverty. In the Puerto Rican mainland communities, there has been a subtle shift (following Black models) from civil rights and integration to an emphasis on Puerto Rican power and community solidarity.

And the Puerto Rican poor in their urban barrios have encountered as their chief adversaries the Black poor in the grim struggle for anti-poverty monies and for the participative identities on Community Action Programs (funded by the Office of Economic Opportunity) which are often the vehicles and leverages of political power in the decaying American cities; additionally, a Puerto Rican professional presence in schools and a myriad of other institutional settings has been thwarted by exiled middle-class Cuban professionals. "Most of the Cubans are an exiled professional middle-class that came to the United States for political reasons. They are lauded and rewarded by the United States government for their rejection of Communism and Fidel Castro. The Cubans lean toward the political right, are fearful of the involvement of masses of poor people. Being middle-class they are familiar with 'the system' and operated successfully in this structure. They are competitive and upwardly mobile. They have little sympathy for the uneducated poor." (Hilda Hidalgo, *The Puerto Ricans of Newark, New Jersey*. Newark: *Aspira*, 1971, p. 14.)

It is hardly strange that the Puerto Rican community has looked to the schools, traditionally the road out of poverty, as affording its best hope for successfully negotiating the challenges of an hostile mainland American milieu.

THE EDUCATIONAL EXPERIENCE OF PUERTO RICANS:
The Bitter Legacy of the Past

The Children of the Past

American schools have always had, as students, children from a wide variety of cultural backgrounds; and the non-English speaking child has been no stranger in American urban classrooms. If we are to understand the problems which Puerto Rican children encounter in mainland schools, it is instructive to look at the experience of other children (non-English speaking and culturally different) in American schools. A huge literature (largely ignored until recently) exists on the children of immigrants in the schools. No document on this earlier experience is more impressive than the *Report of the Immigration Commission* (1911) whose *Report on the Children of Immigrants in Schools* (vols. 29–33) is a vast repository of data on the educational history of the children of the poor and the schools.[7]

---

[7] United States Immigration Commission. *Report of the Immigration Commission,* 41 vols. (Washington: Government Printing Office, 1911). *The Report on the Children of Immigrants in Schools* (vols. 29–33) has been reprinted with an introductory essay by F. Cordasco (Metuchen, N.J.: Scarecrow Reprint Corp., 5 vols., 1970).

By 1911, 57.5% of the children in the public schools of 37 of the largest American cities were of foreign-born parentage; in the parochial schools of 24 of these 37 cities, the children of foreign-born parents constituted 63.5% of the total registration.[8] "To the immigrant child the public elementary school was the first step away from his past, a means by which he could learn to assume the characteristics necessary for the long climb upward." [9] And by 1911, almost 50% of the students in secondary schools were of foreign-born parentage.[10] In American cities, the major educational challenge and responsibility was the immigrant child.

In the effort to respond to the needs of the immigrant child, it is important to note that no overall programs were developed to aid any particular immigrant group. Although there was little agreement as to what Americanization was, the schools were committed to Americanize (and to Anglicize) their charges. Ellwood P. Cubberley's *Changing Conceptions of Education* (1909), which Lawrence A. Cremin characterizes as "a typical progressive tract of the era," [11] saw the immigrants as "illiterate, docile, lacking in self-reliance and initiative, and not possessing the Anglo-teutonic conceptions of law, order, and government . . . ," and the school's role was (in Cubberley's view) "to assimilate and amalgamate."

What efforts were made to respond to the needs of immigrant children were improvised, most often directly in answer to specific problems; almost never was any attempt made to give the school and its program a community orientation. The children literally left at the door of the school their language, their cultural identities, and their immigrant subcommunity origins.[12] A child's parents had virtually no role in the schools; [13] and the New York City experience was not atypical in its leaving the immigrant child to the discretion of the individual superintendent, a principal, or a teacher.

[8] The U.S. Immigration Commission, *op. cit. Abstracts. The Children of Immigrants in Schools,* vol. II, pp. 1–15.

[9] Alan M. Thomas, "American Education and the Immigrant," *Teachers College Record,* vol. 55 (April 1954), pp. 253–267.

[10] See footnote 8, *supra.*

[11] Lawrence A. Cremin, *The Transformation of the School* (New York: Knopf, 1961). "To Americanize, in this view, was to divest the immigrant of his ethnic character and to inculcate the dominant Anglo-Saxon morality." (*Ibid.*)

[12] See the autobiography of Leonard Covello, *The Heart Is the Teacher* (New York: McGraw-Hill, 1958). It is significant to note that Covello, as an immigrant boy in East Harlem, was more influenced by the work of the evangelist, Anna C. Ruddy, who had devoted years to social work in the East Harlem Italian community, than by the public schools. See Anna C. Ruddy (pseudonym, Christian McLeod), *The Heart of the Stranger* (New York: Fleming H. Revell, 1908) ; see also Selma Berrol, "Immigrants at School: New York City, 1900–1910," *Urban Education,* vol. 4 (October 1969), pp. 220–230.

[13] See Leonard Covello, *The Social Background of the Italo-American Child: A Study of the Southern Italian Mores and Their Effect on the School Situation in Italy and America,* edited and with an introduction by F. Cordasco (Leiden, The Netherlands: E. J. Brill, 1967) ; and also Leonard Covello, "A High School and Its Immigrant Community: A Challenge and an Opportunity," *Journal of Educational Sociology,* vol. 9 (February 1936), pp. 331–346. "Where the Italian community was studied, it was subjected to the ministrations of social workers (who concentrated on the sociopathology inevitable in a matrix of deprivation and cultural conflict) or to the probing of psychologists who sought to discern and understand the dynamics of adjustment." F. Cordasco, *Italians in the United States* (New York: Oriole Editions, 1972), p. xiii.

Against such a lack of understanding and coordinated effort in behalf of the children of the poor it is hardly strange that the general malaise of the schools was nowhere more symptomatic than in the pervasive phenomenon of the overage pupil who was classed under the rubric "retardation" with all of its negative connotations. The Immigration Commission of 1911 found that the percentage of retardation for the New York City elementary school pupils was 36.4 with the maximum retardation (48.8%) in the fifth grade.[14] The Commission observed:

. . . thus in the third grade the pupils range in age from 5 to 18 years. In similar manner pupils of the age of 14 years are found in every grade from the first of the elementary schools to the last of the high schools. It will, however, be noted that in spite of this divergence the great body of the pupils of a given grade are of certain definite ages, the older and younger pupils being in each case much less numerically represented. It may, therefore, be assumed that there is an appropriate age for each grade. This assumption is the cardinal point in current educational discussion in regard to retardation. If it were assumed that there is a normal age for each grade, then the pupils can be divided into two classes—those who are of normal age or less and those who are above the normal age. The latter or overage pupils are designated as "retarded."[15]

At best, it is a dismal picture whose poignant and evocative pathos is etched in the faces of the children imprisoned in the cheerless classrooms of the era.[16] It could have been otherwise: in the lower East Side of New York City the efforts of District School Superintendent, Julia Richman, at the turn of the century, pointed in the more rewarding directions of community awareness, of building on the cultural strengths which the child brought to the school; and the near quarter-century tenure (1934–1957) of Leonard Covello at Benjamin Franklin High School in New York City's East Harlem, dramatically underscored the successes of the community centered school. But Julia Richman and Leonard Covello were the exceptions, not the rule; and it is hardly fortuitous that they came out of the emerging Jewish and Italian subcommunities, for these very identities help explain their responsiveness to the immigrant child.[17]

[14] United States Immigration Commission. *The Children of Immigrants in Schools, op. cit.,* vol. 32, p. 609.

[15] *Ibid.,* pp. 608–609.

[16] See many of the contemporary photographs taken by the social reformer Jacob Riis and reproduced in his books, particularly, *The Children of the Poor* (New York: Scribner, 1892); and, generally, in F. Cordasco, ed., *Jacob Riis Revisited: Poverty and the Slum in Another Era* (New York: Doubleday, 1968). See also Robert Hunter, *Poverty* [particularly the chapter entitled, "The Child"] (New York: Macmillan, 1904); and John Spargo, *The Bitter Cry of the Children* (New York: Macmillan, 1907).

[17] Julia Richman has, unfortunately, been neglected; she is one of the great urban school reformers in a period marked by hostility and contempt for the children of the poor. All of her writings are important. See particularly the following: "A Successful Experiment in Promoting Pupils," *Educational Review,* vol. 18 (June 1899), pp. 23–29; "The Incorrigible Child," *Educational Review,* vol. 31 (May 1906), pp. 484–506; "The Social Needs of the Public Schools," *Forum,* vol. 43 (February 1910), pp. 161–169; "What Can Be Done for the Backward Child," *The Survey,* vol. 13 (November 1904), pp. 129–131. For Covello, see footnote #13, *supra;* and his "A Community Centered School

PUERTO RICAN CHILDREN IN THE SCHOOLS

The Early Years

It is in the perspectives of these earlier experiences that the educational failures of the Puerto Rican child are to be viewed and understood. Committed to policies of Americanization, the schools neglected the cultural heritage of the Puerto Rican child, rejected his ancestral language, and generally ignored his parents and community. And these policies were in keeping with the traditional practices of the schools.

The Puerto Rican community in New York City is the largest on the mainland, and its experience would be essentially typical of other mainland urban communities. As early as 1938, the difficulties of the Puerto Rican child in the New York City schools are graphically (if passingly) noted:

Many Puerto Rican children who enter the public schools in New York speak or understand little English. The children who are transferred from schools in Puerto Rico to those in New York are usually put back in their classes so that they are with children who are two or three years younger than they are. Americans who are teaching Puerto Rican children express the opinion that these children have had less training in discipline and in group cooperation than American children. Lacking the timidity of many of the children in this country, they sometimes act in an unrestrained and impulsive manner. One large agency in the settlement, which has dealt with Puerto Rican children for many years, reported that under proper conditions Puerto Rican children are responsive, easily managed, and affectionate. In contrast to this, another large institution said that for some reason which they could not explain the Puerto Rican children were more destructive than any group of children with whom they had had contact. All the evidence obtainable shows the relation of unsatisfactory home conditions to difficulties at school. During the past few years the desperate economic condition of these families has caused them to move so frequently that it has often been difficult to locate the children when they did not attend school.[18]

In December, 1946, Dr. Paul Kennedy, then President of the New York City Association of Assistant Superintendents, appointed a committee "to study and report on the educational adjustments made necessary by the addition of the 400,000 Puerto Ricans who have lately become residents

and the Problem of Housing," *Educational Forum*, vol. 7 (January 1943); and "A Principal Speaks to His Community," *American Unity*, vol. 2 (May 1944).

[18] Lawrence R. Chenault, *The Puerto Rican Migrant in New York City*. With a Foreword by F. Cordasco (New York: Russell & Russell, 1970), p. 146. See also C. P. Armstrong, *Reactions of Puerto Rican Children in New York City to Psychological Tests. A Report of the Special Committee on Immigration and Naturalization* (State of New York: Chamber of Commerce, 1935) which Chenault used but (in keeping with the temper of the time) noted, "It is not the purpose of this study to raise the question of the innate ability of the migrant." Perhaps, the earliest notice of Puerto Ricans in New York City is the unpublished typescript (14 pp.) on file in the office of the National Urban League, William E. Hill, *Porto Rican Colonies in New York* (1929).

of this city." The surprisingly comprehensive report prepared by this committee considered native backgrounds; migration to the mainland; problems of assimilation; the education of the Puerto Rican pupil; and made a number of recommendations.[19] That the report was anchored in the past is evident in its caution that "Although the Puerto Rican is an American citizen, the adjustment he must make in this city is like that of immigrants to this country from a foreign land." The report counted "13,914 pupils enrolled [June 1947; by October 1970, 260,040 were enrolled] in the public elementary and junior high schools of the city who originally came from Puerto Rico"; and further grimly observed: "there is no doubt but that many pupils coming from Puerto Rico suffer from the double handicap of unfamiliarity with the English language and lack of previous educational experience, sometimes approaching complete illiteracy. Malnutrition and other health deficiencies contribute to the educational problem of the schools. The overcrowding at home and the restlessness on the street carry over into the school in the form of nervousness, extreme shyness, near tantrums, and other behavior characteristics which are the more difficult for the teacher to understand because of the language barrier." (p. 38)

The Committee also undertook the first study of "reading progress" among Puerto Rican pupils who were new admissions to the elementary and junior high schools; and it made a series of recommendations, chief among which was the establishment of special classes ("C" classes) for Puerto Rican children "for whom at least a year's time is needed for preliminary instruction and language work before they are ready for complete assimilation in the regular program." Although the report was generally neglected, it represented the first systematic study undertaken on the mainland to call attention to the needs of Puerto Rican children.

Attention has been called to J. J. Osuna's *Report on Visits to New York City Schools* in 1948 (see footnote #3). In 1951, a Mayor's Committee on Puerto Rican Affairs in New York City was convened and considered the needs of Puerto Rican pupils; [20] and in 1953, Dr. Leonard Covello, then Principal of Benjamin Franklin High School in East Harlem, consolidated and articulated into schematic form for consideration the various proposals which had been made up to that time to deal with the needs of Puerto Rican children in the schools.[21]

[19] *A Program of Education for Puerto Ricans in New York City. A Report Prepared by a Committee of the Association of Assistant Superintendents* (New York: Board of Education, 1947). The report (106 pp.) was mimeographed with what appears to be a very limited circulation. "For years, boys and girls from Puerto Rico have entered the public schools of New York City. For the most part they came into Spanish Harlem, arriving in such small numbers that their admission to school was accepted routinely. Together with other non-English speaking children from European countries, they were placed in 'C' classes, and gradually assimilated into the regular program of the school. There was no reference then to a 'Puerto Rican problem' in the schools." (p. 3)

[20] "Puerto Rican Pupils in American Schools." *Mayor's Committee on Puerto Rican Affairs in New York City. Report of the Subcommittee on Education, Recreation and Parks* (New York: 1951). Part of the report is reprinted in Cordasco and Bucchioni, *op. cit.*, pp. 246–253.

[21] Leonard Covello, "Recommendations Concerning Puerto Rican Pupils in Our Public Schools" (Benjamin Franklin High School, May 1, 1953). This is an invaluable document, and is published

Finally, in 1953, the New York City Board of Education presented in booklet form the results of a study initiated by its Division of Curriculum Development. This brief report indicated a new awareness of the importance of using Spanish in instructing Puerto Rican children, of the need for knowledge of Puerto Rican cultural backgrounds, and of the need for bilingual teachers.[22] But it equally made clear the critical need for a fully developed educational program for Puerto Rican children; and it served as a prologue to the *Puerto Rican Study* which was initiated in 1953.

THE PUERTO RICAN STUDY

The *Puerto Rican Study*, which is here re-published in a new edition, was, for its time, one of the most generously funded educational studies.[23] The Fund for the Advancement of Education provided a grant-in-aid of a half million dollars and "contributions equivalent in amounts authorized by the Board of Education made the study a vital operation in the school system." (*Foreword*) It was not completed until 1957, and it was finally published in April 1959. It is, unquestionably, the fullest study ever made of the Puerto Rican educational experience on the mainland; and, in a broader sense, it remains one of the most comprehensive statements yet made, not only of the Puerto Rican school experience, but of the educational experience of the non-English speaking minority child in the American school.[24] As such it is an invaluable document in American educational historiography, with all of the contemporary relevancies which the 1960s have defined (and continuing into the 1970s) with reference to ethnicity, the minority child, the contexts of poverty, and the educational needs of the "disadvantaged" child. It is strange that, in the proliferating literature on the minority child and the schools, *The Puerto Rican Study* should have been neglected; and its neglect may be due to its appearance before the advent of the Johnsonian anti-poverty programs of the 1960s with their

in Cordasco and Bucchioni, *op. cit.,* pp. 254–259. Attention should also be called to *Education of the Non-English Speaking and Bilingual (Spanish) Pupils in the Junior High Schools of Districts 10 and 11, Manhattan* (June 1952), prepared at the request of New York City Assistant Superintendent Clare C. Baldwin. The report noted that "every school in Districts 10 and 11 has some Puerto Rican children on its register."

22 *Teaching Children of Puerto Rican Background in New York City Schools* (New York: Board of Education, 1953).

23 For some of the backgrounds of the report, see J. Cayce Morrison, *A Letter to Friends of Puerto Rican Children* (1955); and his "The Puerto Rican Study—What It Is; Where It Is Going," *Journal of Educational Sociology,* vol. 28 (December 1954), pp. 167–173.

24 The only comparable work is Leonard Covello's *The Social Background of the Italo-American School Child* (see footnote #13). For the contiguity and relationships of the Italian and Puerto Rican communities in East Harlem, see F. Cordasco and R. Galattioto, "Ethnic Displacement in the Interstitial Community: The East Harlem (New York City) Experience," *Phylon: The Atlanta University Review of Race & Culture,* vol. 31 (Fall 1970), pp. 302–312. *The Puerto Rican Study* was released officially by the New York City Board of Education on April 6, 1959. See *New York Times,* April 7, 1959. "Dr. John J. Theobold, The Superintendent of Schools, said that a 'substantial number' of recommendations and findings in the study had already been implemented. Teaching materials, courses of study and guides developed by the project, he said, are now being used. He said there were now 2,255 special classes for Puerto Rican children in the elementary and 346 such classes in the secondary schools." *New York Times, loc. cit.*

educational components, and to the inevitable fate of sponsored reports whose implementation and evaluation are seldom realized or avoided for a variety of reasons.

The Puerto Rican Study's objectives are clearly stated:

In a narrow sense, *The Puerto Rican Study* was a four-year inquiry into the education and adjustment of Puerto Rican pupils in the public schools of the City of New York. In a broader sense, it was a major effort of the school authorities to establish on a sound basis a city-wide program for the continuing improvement of the educational opportunities of all non-English-speaking pupils in the public schools.

While the *Study* was focused on the public schools in New York City, it was planned and conducted in the belief that the findings might be useful to all schools, public and private, that are trying to serve children from a Spanish-language culture. As the *Study* developed, it seemed apparent that it might have values, direct or indirect, wherever children are being taught English as a second language. (p. 1)

It sought answers to the following specific problems: (1) What are the most effective methods and materials for teaching English as a second language to newly arrived Puerto Rican pupils? (2) What are the most effective techniques whereby the school can promote a more rapid and more effective adjustment of Puerto Rican parents and children to the community and of the community to them?

As the *Study* progressed, its staff developed two series of related curriculum bulletins—*Resource Units* organized around themes and designed for all pupils, and a *Language Guide Series* which provided the content and methods for adapting the instruction to the needs of the pupils learning English (the *Study* lists the *Units* and *Series*). The *Study* also furnished a detailed description of the Puerto Rican children; devised a scale to rate English-speaking ability; and constructed a detailed program for the in-service education of teachers (Chapter 17).[25]

25 *The Resource Units* and the *Language Guide Series* are invaluable aids for the teacher who is looking for materials for the instructional program for Puerto Rican children; equally valuable (and developed as part of *The Puerto Rican Study*) is Samuel M. Goodman, *Tests and Testing: Developing a Program for Testing Puerto Rican Pupils in Mainland Schools* (New York: Board of Education, 1958). Admittedly, *The Resource Units* and the *Language Guide Series* were intended (in their emphases) to facilitate a more rapid adjustment to the American way of life (in keeping with the ethos of *The Puerto Rican Study* and its period), but this does not detract from their value as cognitive aids. *The Puerto Rican Study* and its ancillary materials are a complete conspectus for the education of Puerto Rican children measured against the principles discussed in Theodore Andersson and Mildred Boyer, *Bilingual Schooling in the United States,* 2 vols. (Austin, Texas: Southwest Educational Development Laboratory, 1970); and Vera P. John and Vivian M. Horner, *Early Childhood Bilingual Education* (New York: Modern Language Association of America, 1971). Notice should also be made of the materials describing the programs at the Bilingual School (Public School #211, Bronx, N.Y.) which incorporate many of the recommendations of *The Puerto Rican Study*. The most completely developed Bilingual School in the United States is Public School #25 (Bronx, N.Y.) whose programs are essentially based on the recommendations of *The Puerto Rican Study*.

The Recommendations of

THE PUERTO RICAN STUDY

Its recommendations ("Where *The Puerto Rican Study* Leads") are both a blueprint and design for effectively meeting the needs of Puerto Rican children, and they impinge on all those facets of the experience of the minority child which are interrelated and which, if neglected, impede social growth and cognitive achievement. Simply listed (without the capsuled rationales which accompany them), they represent a skeletal construct as meaningful today as when they were formulated:

1. Accept *The Puerto Rican Study,* not as something finished, but as the first stage of a larger, city-wide, ever improving program for the education and assimilation of non-English-speaking children.
2. Take a new look at the philosophy governing the education of the non-English-speaking children in New York City schools.
3. Recognize that whatever is done for the non-English-speaking child is, in the long run, done for all the children.
4. Use the annual school census as a basic technic in planning the continuing adaptation of the schools to the needs of the non-English-speaking pupils.
5. Recognize the heterogeneity of the non-English-speaking pupils.
6. Formulate a uniform policy for the reception, screening, placement, and periodic assessment of non-English-speaking pupils.
7. Keep policies governing the grouping of non-English-speaking pupils flexible. Place the emphasis upon serving the needs of the individual pupil.
8. Place special emphasis on reducing the backlog of retarded language learners.
9. Recognize "English as a second language" or "the teaching of non-English-speaking children" as an area of specialization that cuts across many subject areas.
10. Use the curricular materials developed by *The Puerto Rican Study* to achieve unity of purpose and practice in teaching non-English-speaking pupils.
11. Capitalize on the creative talent of teachers in finding ways and means of supplementing and of improving the program for teaching non-English-speaking pupils.
12. Recognize and define the school's responsibility to assist, counsel, and cooperate with the parents of non-English-speaking pupils in all matters pertaining to the child's welfare.
13. Take a new look at the school's opportunity to accelerate the adjustment of Puerto Rican children and their parents through advice and counsel to parents on problems normally considered to be outside the conventional functions of the school.
14. Staff the schools to do the job: to help the new arrival to make good adjustment to school and community; to help the non-English-speaking

child to learn English and to find his way successfully into the main stream of the school's program.

15. Staff the proper agencies of the Board of Education to maintain a continuing program for the development and improvement of curricular materials and other aids to the teaching of non-English-speaking pupils.

16. Staff, also, the proper agencies of the Board of Education, and set in motion the processes to maintain a continuing assessment or evaluation of technics, practices and proposals.

17. Take a new hard look at the psychological services provided for non-English-speaking children, especially for Puerto Rican children.

18. Through every means available, make it clear that the education of the non-English-speaking children and their integration in an ever changing school population is the responsibility of every member of the school staff.

19. Maintain, improve, and possibly expand the program of in-service preparation initiated through *The Puerto Rican Study* for training special staff to assist in accelerating the program for non-English-speaking children.

20. In cooperation with the colleges and universities of Metropolitan New York, create a dynamic program to achieve unity of purpose and more adequate coordination of effort in the education of teachers and of other workers for accelerating the program in the schools.

21. Use the varied opportunities available to develop an ever improving cooperation between the Department of Education in Puerto Rico and the Board of Education in New York City.

22. In cooperation with the responsible representatives of the government of the State of New York, continue to explore the mutual interests and responsibility of the city and the state for the education and adjustment of non-English-speaking children and youth.

23. Think of the City of New York and the Commonwealth of Puerto Rico as partners in a great enterprise.

No full scale implementation of *The Puerto Rican Study* was attempted. Much of what the *Study* recommended appears again in the New York City Board of Education *Educating Students for whom English is a Second Language: Programs, Activities, and Services* (1965), a pamphlet-review of subsequent programs which emphasized teacher training programs, particularly the exchange of teachers between New York and Puerto Rico. All kinds of reasons can be advanced for the failure to implement *The Puerto Rican Study,* and these might include teacher and Board of Education resistance; the struggles which were to ensue over community participation, and decentralization; the rapidly politicizing community/school contexts with their attendant ideological quarrels; the absence of qualified personnel; and the accelerating growth of the Puerto Rican community which simply overwhelmed many of the schools. Whatever the reasons (and no one reason or a combination of reasons provides an acceptable explanation), the *Study* remains one of the most important educational investigations ever undertaken. Its achievements (however incompletely implemented) included the following:

1. Developed two series of related curriculum bulletins—*Resource Units* and *Language Guides*—for use in teaching English to non-English-speaking pupils. These are keyed to New York City courses of study but may be easily adapted to courses of study in other school systems. They are adapted to the maturity level of children, grade by grade in the elementary school, and in terms of need for special instruction in English during the early secondary school years.

2. Developed a guide for teaching science—resource units and sample lessons—to Puerto Rican pupils who are still trying to learn English; and a guide for teaching occupations to teen-age Puerto Rican pupils in high school who wish to qualify for occupational employment.

3. Developed a battery of tests, measures, and data-gathering technics for use with Puerto Rican pupils in the mainland schools. Among these were a tape-recorded test for measuring the ability of non-English-speaking pupils to understand spoken English, a scale for rating ability to speak English, a bilingual test of arithmetic, and a process for screening new arrivals and for following their progress through periodic reviews.

4. Through an educational-ethnic-social survey of several thousand children in New York City elementary and junior high schools, obtained a profile of the characteristics of pupils of Puerto Rican background in relation to other pupils in the same grades and schools.

5. Through testing thousands of pupils, obtained estimates of the potential abilities as well as of the present performance of Puerto Rican pupils in relation to their peers, *i.e.*, other pupils of the same age and grade in the same schools.

6. Through a variety of studies of individual children from kindergarten through the tenth grade or second year of high school, gained revealing information concerning the problems of Puerto Rican children in achieving cultural-educational-social adjustment in New York City schools.

7. Through a survey of the relations of schools to Puerto Rican parents, defined the problems confronting the schools, formulated criteria for determining the schools' role, and made some estimate of the cost in terms of personnel needed to help facilitate or accelerate the cultural adjustment of Puerto Rican parents.

8. Through analysis of previously established positions and of new positions established on an experimental basis, developed criteria for determining the necessity for special staff in schools to enable them to serve the needs of Puerto Rican and foreign-born or non-English-speaking children.

9. Through two years of experimentation with different procedures, developed proposals for an in-service program to reach all teachers required to teach non-English-speaking pupils.

10. Through participation in three summer workshops sponsored in part by the Board of Education of the City of New York at the University of Puerto Rico, formulated proposals for the development of the annual workshop as a continuing means of promoting better mutual understanding and cooperation between the school system of New York City and the school system of Puerto Rico.

11. Through the surveys and testing of thousands of children, devised a plan for obtaining a uniform census of all Puerto Rican and foreign-born children in the schools. Administration of census, through consecutive years, will give the Board of Education data for predicting with a high degree of accuracy pending changes in the ethnic composition of pupil population by school, school district, school level, borough and city.

12. The gradation of ability to speak English as defined by the Puerto Rican Study in its scale for rating ability to speak English was used by the Commissioner of Education of the State of New York in defining non-English-speaking pupils as a basis for the distribution of additional state aid appropriated by law. (pp. 9–10)

In themselves, these achievements (and the recommendations) were to become the measuring criteria against which continuing needs were to be delineated.[26]

BEYOND THE PUERTO RICAN STUDY:
The Bilingual Education Act

Much of the effort in behalf of the educational needs of Puerto Rican children in the 1960s must be viewed and understood in the light of the

---

[26] The failure to implement *The Puerto Rican Study* led to great agitation and continuing demands from the Puerto Rican community. The first Citywide Conference of the Puerto Rican Community (April 1967) in its published proceedings (*Puerto Ricans Confront Problems of the Complex Urban Society*, New York City: Office of the Mayor, 1968) presented recommendations for the education of Puerto Rican children, essentially a repetition of those made by *The Puerto Rican Study*. And in 1968, Aspira (an organization founded in 1961 by the Puerto Rican Forum to promote higher education for Puerto Ricans) convened a national conference of Puerto Ricans, Mexican-Americans, and educators on "The Special Educational Needs of Urban Puerto Rican Youth." The conference's published report (*Hemos Trabajado Bien,* New York: Aspira, 1968), in its recommendations, reiterated most of those of *The Puerto Rican Study*. The Aspira conference also commissioned a report on Puerto Ricans and the public schools, Richard J. Margolis, *The Losers: A Report on Puerto Ricans and the Public Schools* (New York: Aspira, 1968). This brief report chronicles visits to sixteen schools in seven cities and "makes no explicit recommendations. Its purpose is to put the problem in sharper focus and on wider display, not to promote any single set of solutions." Margolis' report is a devastating indictment of those schools which neglected Puerto Rican children, and of programs which largely were encrusted with all the bitter abuses of the past: it appears inconceivable that the practices he describes could have been occurring a decade after the publication of *The Puerto Rican Study*.

massive federal interventions in education largely initiated by the enactment of the Elementary & Secondary Education Act of 1965, and its
subsequent amendments.

The passage by the Congress in 1968 of the Bilingual Education Act
(itself, Title VII of the ESEA) reaffirmed and strengthened many of the
recommendations of *The Puerto Rican Study*, even though the *Study* had
largely fallen into undeserved neglect. The struggle for a national bilingual
education act represented a continuing fight against the ethnocentric
rejection of the use of native languages in the instruction of non-English-
speaking children; [27] and, in our view, the successful enactment of the
Bilingual Education Act represented a movement away from the "ethnocentric illusion" in the United States that for a child born in this country
English is not a foreign language, and virtually all instruction in schools
must be through the medium of English; even more importantly, the Act
was a national manifesto for cultural pluralism and bicultural education,
and in this sense may prove the most socially significant educational legislation yet enacted.

The Act recognized "the special education needs of the large numbers
of children of limited English speaking ability in the United States," and
declared "it to be the policy of the United States to provide financial
assistance to local educational agencies to develop and carry out new and
imaginative elementary and secondary school programs designed to meet
these special educational needs." The main priorities of the Act are the
provision of equal educational opportunities for non-English-speaking
children; the strengthening of educational programs for bilingual children;
and the promotion of bilingualism among all students. A great number of
programs have come into being as a result of the Act, and although the
programs are of differing (and in some instances of dubious) quality, they
affirm the practicability of meeting the needs of the non-English-speaking
child. [28] Use of the principles and recommendations of *The Puerto Rican
Study* would strengthen programs for Puerto Rican children, as even a
casual examination would affirm.

THE REALITIES OF PROGRAM IMPLEMENTATION

In the last analysis, it is the program which addresses itself to the
educational needs of the Puerto Rican child which must be evaluated with
recommendations made for its continuing improvement. The evaluation of
a particular program for Puerto Rican children in a large urban school

[27] See F. Cordasco, "The Challenge of the non-English-Speaking Child in American Schools,"
School & Society, vol. 96 (March 30, 1968), pp. 198–201, which is an adaptation of testimony before
the Committee on Education and Labor of the U.S. House of Representatives in support of the proposed Title VII (June 29, 1967) ; and for the history of the legislation, see F. Cordasco, "Educational Enlightenment Out of Texas: Toward Bilingualism," *Teachers College Record,* vol. 71 (May
1970), pp. 608–612; and F. Cordasco, "The Bilingual Education Act," *Phi Delta Kappan,* vol. 51
(October 1969), p. 75. The Bilingual Education Act, Title VII (P.L. 90–247; 20 U.S.C. 880b)
authorized the expenditure of $25 million in Fiscal 1971.

[28] For a list and description of some of the programs, see "Bilingualism," *The Center Forum,*
vol. 4 (September 1969), pp. 20–26; and Vera P. John and Vivian M. Horner, *op. cit.,* pp. 15–107.

district and the recommendations which were made for its improvement and expansion are, in themselves, instructive: they delineate the contemporary educational experience for the Puerto Rican child, and they point the way to meeting the needs.

The recommendations which are subjoined derive from a study and evaluation of the educational programs for Puerto Rican students underway in the Jersey City (N.J.) school district in 1971–1972.[29] Over 5,000 Puerto Rican pupils (out of a total school register of some 38,000) were in the city's schools. The recommendations provide a profile of contemporary Puerto Rican educational experience (practice that lends itself to improvement), generally encountered on the mainland.

PROGRAM RECOMMENDATIONS:
Elementary Level

1. The basic recommendation to be made for the elementary schools involves the establishment of functional bilingual programs wherever there are Puerto Rican students in attendance. The basic premise of bilingual education involves the use of Spanish to provide instruction in most curriculum areas when English is not the mother tongue of the children and when there is insufficient fluency in English to profit from school instruction in that language. Thus, for example, instruction in basic curriculum areas such as mathematics, social studies, etc. would be in Spanish. At the same time that instruction is given in the basic content areas in Spanish, an intensive program in the teaching of English as a second language must be conducted. As children develop greater fluency in English, add'tional instruction in the basic curriculum areas should be given in English. This approach would assist children in becoming equally fluent in both Spanish and English, and at the same time it would also assist children to develop the appropriate knowledges and skills in curriculum areas other than Spanish and English. Bilingual education should also provide for the teaching of Spanish as a second language for those children who are dominant in English. Such programs should begin in September 1972.

At the present time in the bilingual classes in the Jersey City schools, this approach is not in widespread use. Teachers who speak Spanish are used for the most part to interpret what the English speaking teacher has said, and (as noted above) often at the same time, a practice resulting in considerable confusion. In addition, the practice of assigning two teachers to a room, one of whom functions as an interpreter, represents poor utilization of personnel, both educationally and financially.

2. The bilingual program recommended by the evaluators would also necessitate the regrouping of participating children more carefully.`In

---

29 F. Cordasco and Eugene Bucchioni, *Education Programs for Puerto Rican Students: Evaluation and Recommendations* (Jersey City: Board of Education, 1971), pp. 27–37.

addition to using the traditional criteria for grouping, in a bilingual education program it is necessary to develop parallel classes or sections of children who are dominant in either English or Spanish. In developing bilingual programs, however, it is essential that priority be given in class assignment to children who are dominant in Spanish, rather than to those dominant in English, because the greatest immediate need exists for children who are dominant in Spanish and who cannot derive as much educational value as possible from school programs conducted solely in English.

3. It is recommended that two schools [perhaps, Public School No. 2 and Public School No. 16 in view of the very large number of Puerto Rican students in attendance] develop complete bilingual programs beginning with the kindergarten and including each grade in the school. In other schools, bilingual classes should be established as needed.

4. A committee on bilingual education at the elementary school level should be established immediately in order to plan for the development of bilingual programs in Public Schools Nos. 2 and 16, and in other schools of Jersey City where there are large Puerto Rican enrollments. The bilingual education committee will also give attention to the development of a bilingual curriculum encompassing the usual curriculum areas as well as the teaching of English as a second language, the teaching of Spanish as a second language, and the history and culture of Puerto Rico as an integral part of the elementary school curriculum. The present Hispanic Culture Committee is a beginning; but it must deal with a Puerto Rican studies curriculum and only ancillarily with Hispanic cultures in general. Membership on the committee should include parents, teachers, principals and should also make provision for student input.

5. A city wide Puerto Rican advisory council composed of parents, high school and college students and community leaders should be established. The advisory council can advise school officials on the needs, aspirations, sentiments and responses of the Puerto Rican community insofar as educational matters are concerned. The existence of a community advisory council will assist in making public schools with large numbers of Puerto Rican students "community schools," furnishing educational and other much needed services to the Puerto Rican community. Such an advisory council on a city wide basis [and articulated with local advisory councils for specific schools] will provide much needed community participation in education in Jersey City for the Puerto Rican community.

6. Parochial schools with large numbers of Puerto Rican students should also participate in special programs funded with federal monies.

7. All communications from school officials to parents should be available in both English and Spanish.

8. Additional Puerto Rican personnel should be recruited for positions at all levels in the public schools including teachers, principals, school secretaries, a curriculum specialist, teacher aides, etc. Special attention should be turned immediately to the employment of a curriculum specialist in bilingual education.

9. At the present time, no city-wide coordinating effort involving existing bilingual programs is available in Jersey City. It is recommended, therefore, that a city wide office at the level of coordinator for bilingual education be established. This office will have jurisdiction over planning, developing, implementing, supervising and evaluating all bilingual education programs, programs in the teaching of English as a second language, and other special service programs for Puerto Rican elementary school children and high school students. The office would also provide liaison with the Puerto Rican community.

10. Bilingual classes as envisaged in recommendation #1 should also be made available in the Summer of 1972. [The period January 1972 to June 1972 should be used as a planning period for the bilingual programs to be established in the Summer and Fall of 1972.]

11. It is recommended that provision be made for the establishment of a continuing consultancy in the implementation of the recommendations contained in this report. Consultants would work with school officials and members of the Puerto Rican community in the implementation of the recommendations and would assist in the development of other programs and special services that may be needed by the children of the Puerto Rican community.

12. Parent education programs conducted in both Spanish and English should be developed for the Puerto Rican community.

13. An in-service program for teachers and other school personnel should be developed as soon as possible. Current and past efforts in Jersey City in the areas of in-service courses include the offering of a course in "Teaching English as a Second Language" that was to be given in the 1970/71 school year, beginning in November, 1970 and a request to develop and finance an "In-Service Course Involving Philosophy, Approaches and Methodology of Bilingual Education," to be given during the 1971/72 school year. In-service efforts should be expanded, and should include both professionals participating directly in bilingual programs or English as a second language programs as well as other professionals in the Jersey City Public Schools who may not be participating in special programs for Puerto Rican children but who do work with Puerto Rican children in regular classes. Such an extensive in-service program might be developed and offered during the regular school year, or might be given as a special summer institute for participating personnel.

14. Greater numbers of Puerto Rican student teachers should be recruited from Jersey City State College. An expanded student-teaching practicum drawn from the cadres of Puerto Rican students at Jersey City State College represents an important source for recruiting larger numbers of Puerto Rican personnel for employment in the Jersey City Public Schools.

15. A continuing and expanded liaison between the Jersey City Public Schools and Jersey City State College is recommended. Here, an important beginning and model [Title VII, at School No. 16] has been provided by Professor Bloom and Jersey City State College personnel.

Secondary Level

1. The city-wide Community Advisory Council described in recommendations for elementary schools would also turn its attention to secondary education and make recommendations relevant to the educational needs of Puerto Rican high school students in Jersey City.

2. A testing and identification program should be developed at the secondary level. Such a program would attempt to identify Puerto Rican students in need of intensive instruction in English as a second language or in other important school subjects such as reading.

3. A special committee to deal with secondary education for Puerto Rican students should be established, with the membership drawn from teachers, principals, guidance personnel and other school professionals; and including parents and students from the Puerto Rican community. The committee should give special attention to the current basic offerings: industrial arts, college preparatory, business and general studies. It should consider ways of increasing the holding power of the secondary schools so that greater numbers of Puerto Rican students remain in high school and graduate.

4. Special work study programs for Puerto Rican students might be developed in connection with the basic offerings now available. Such work study programs could become a very significant phase of the industrial arts and business education programs, and should, consequently, carry high school credit.

5. An immediate attempt should be made to increase the number of Puerto Rican students in the college preparatory program. This can be done by teachers, guidance personnel and administrators. More information about current high school programs should be made available, and students should become familiar with the implications of selecting specific programs and the out-of-school consequences of enrollment in any given program. In addition, talent-search programs might be initiated to increase the number of Puerto Rican students entering college.

6. Secondary school teachers should participate in in-service programs dealing with the education of Puerto Rican students.

7. It is recommended that high school students having little fluency in English be given basic instruction in Spanish in the various classes required in the four curricula. Instruction in Spanish would be in addition to intensive instruction in reading, writing and speaking English as a second language. When high school students have achieved a sufficient degree of fluency in English, they may then receive all or most of their instruction in English. Bilingual education at the high school level at the present time is essential, and it is especially important when large numbers of students are dominant in Spanish rather than in English. It should be remembered that it was not possible to secure from school officials data concerning the number of Puerto Rican high school students dominant primarily in Spanish.

8. At present, a secondary school curriculum committee is working on a course of study in Puerto Rican history. The work of this committee

should be accelerated and a course of study in Puerto Rican history and culture should be developed as rapidly as possible. The committee might then turn its attention to the development of a course of study dealing with the Puerto Rican experience on the mainland. At present, there are no student members of this committee. Students should be a significant and contributing part of this committee. Indeed, greater participation by high school students in the decisions affecting their school careers is vital, and it becomes especially crucial when there are large numbers of students dropping out of high school programs as is true for many Puerto Rican students.

9. The high schools should make available to all high school students without cost all special examinations such as the National Education Development Tests or the College Boards. Such examinations now require the payment of fees by candidates taking them. There may be many Puerto Rican and other students unable to take the examinations which require the payment of fees because of inability to afford the funds required.

10. The continuing consultancy referred to in recommendations for elementary schools should encompass secondary education as well as elementary education.

11. It is recommended that an experimental program involving independent study be instituted for those students who are considering leaving high school before graduation. This program would provide the opportunity for independent study under supervision, for which credit leading to a high school diploma would be given. Such a program would also provide for attendance in organized classes in the high schools, especially where remedial or advanced programs are required. Students would participate in developing their programs. Such supervised independent study programs could be related to jobs which students leaving high school before graduation may have secured.

12. It is recommended that additional Puerto Rican personnel be recruited for employment in Jersey City secondary schools. The two Puerto Rican guidance counselors at Ferris High School are an important beginning.

These recommendations are, essentially, reaffirmations of the cogency of those made earlier in *The Puerto Rican Study*. One cannot help but wonder how differently meaningful educational opportunity for Puerto Rican children may have been had *The Puerto Rican Study* been implemented. In its cautions and admonitions, *The Puerto Rican Study* was prophetic: "At the very best it will take three to five years to translate the proposals of *The Puerto Rican Study* into an effective program. . . . The real question is, how rapidly can the school system move? . . . there are thousands of Puerto Rican children in New York City schools who have been here two, three, four or more years and are still rated as language learners. The task is twofold—to salvage as many as possible of those currently retarded, and to reduce the numbers that thus far have been added annually to the list. The time to begin is now—A year gone from a child's life is gone forever." (p. 237)

on, Robert W. Party Politics in Puerto Rico. Stanford, Calif:
Stanford University Press, 1965.

Dorothy D. and James R. Bourne. Thirty years of change in
Puerto Rico: A case study of ten selected rural areas. New
York: Praeger, 1966. Assesses the changes that have taken
place in 10 rural communities as a result of programs planned
and executed by the Puerto Rican government. The areas were
first studied in 1932. Data were gathered by means of extensive
interviewing in the community, and some observation was done
by people involved in the earlier study.

Salvador. Historia de Puerto Rico. New York: D. Appleton, 1904.

John H. Spanish-Speaking Groups in the United States. Duke
University Press, 1954. Includes a sketch of "the Puerto Ricans
in New York" (pp. 156-187). Burma assumes that there is a
fundamental "unity of culture" among diverse groups put together because they speak the same language. In light of the
widely differing historical backgrounds which have given rise to
different cultures among Spanish-speaking groups, the assumption does not seem valid.

ult, Lawrence. The Puerto Rican Migrant in New York City.
Columbia University Press, 1938. Reissued with a New Foreword by F. Cordasco. New York: Russell & Russell, 1970.
The one book that puts together data available on the early
movements to New York City of Puerto Rican migrants. Includes a discussion of the various ways these movements affect
the established community and the migrants.

sco, F. and David Alloway, "Spanish Speaking People in the United
States: Some Research Constructs and Postulates," International Migration Review, vol. 4 (Spring 1970), pp. 76-79.

sco, F. and Eugene Bucchioni. The Puerto Rican Experience: A
Sociological Sourcebook (Totowa, N. J.: Rowman & Littlefield,
1973).

rick, Joseph P. Puerto Rican Americans: The Meaning of Migration to the Mainland. Englewood Cliffs, N.J.: Prentice Hall,
1971. An overview and trenchant study with materials on the
dynamics of migration: the problem of identity; the family;
problem of color; religion; education; welfare. See New York
Times, September 12, 1971, p. 96.

BIBLIOGRAPHY OF SELECTED REFERENCES

Ander

Bourn

BIBLIOGRAPHY OF SELECTED R

I GENERAL BIBLIOGRA

Cordasco, Francesco with Eugene Bucchioni a
Puerto Ricans on the United States Ma
Reports, Texts, Critical Studies and
New Jersey: Rowman & Littlefield, 1
raphy of 754 main entries dealing wit
ces; the migration to the mainland; th
flict and acculturation on the mainlan
land; and social needs encompassing
ment, and other human needs.

Brau,

Burma

Bravo, Enrique R. Bibliografia Puertorriqueñ
New York: Urban Center of Columbi
lish translation by Marcial Cuevas).
of 338 main references, largely of th
predominantly in Spanish.

Cordasco, Francesco and Leonard Covello. S
Children in American Schools: A Pre
New York: Department of Labor, Mi
wealth of Puerto Rico, 1967. (some 4
lished in Education Libraries Bulletin
University of London, #31 (Spring 196
Journal of Human Relations, vol. 16 (

Chena

(Cordasco, Francesco). The People of Puerto
New York: Department of Labor, Mi
monwealth of Puerto Rico (1968). Sor

Corda

Dossick, Jesse. Doctoral Research on Puerto
New York: New York University, Sc
A classified list of 320 doctoral disse
American mainland universities.

Corda

II GENERAL STUDIES

Fitzp

Aïtken, Thomas H., Jr. Poet in the Fortress
can Library, 1964. A biography of L

Glazer, Nathan and Daniel P. Moynihan. "The Puerto Ricans." In: Be-
    yond the Melting Pot: The Negroes, Puerto Ricans, Jews, Ital-
    ians, and Irish of New York City, by Nathan Glazer and Daniel
    Moynihan. Cambridge: M.I.T. and Harvard University Press,
    2nd ed., 1970. Puerto Ricans in New York City are discussed
    in terms of who migrates to the United States; their relation-
    ship to the island of Puerto Rico; business, professional, labor
    opportunities, and average earnings in New York; and the effect
    of migration on the culture of the migrants. The Puerto Ricans
    are compared and contrasted with immigrant groups. (1st ed.,
    1963). The 2nd edition updates some of the material, and in-
    cludes a new introductory essay and analysis.

Howard University. Symposium: Puerto Rico in the Year 2000. Wash-
    ington: University Press, 1968. Eleven papers by Puerto Ri-
    cans and North Americans about the island's past, present,
    and future.

Lewis, Gordon K. Puerto Rico: Freedom and Power in the Caribbean.
    New York: Montly Review Press, 1963. A critical study cover-
    ing Puerto Rico's relations with the United States and its Carib-
    bean neighbors.

Lewis, Oscar. La Vida: A Puerto Rican Family in the Culture of Pov-
    erty -- San Juan and New York. New York: Random House,
    1966. 669 pp. Begins with a long introduction which describes
    Lewis' methods, the setting, and the family involved in the
    study. A discussion of the theory of the "culture of poverty"
    is included. The rest of the book is the story of a Puerto Rican
    family, as told by the members of the nuclear family and some
    of their relatives and friends. See Also Oscar Lewis; A Study
    of Slum Culture: Backgrounds for La Vida. New York: Ran-
    dom House, 1968. Provides the general background, data, and
    statistical frame of reference for La Vida.

McKown, Robin, Image of Puerto Rico. With a Foreword by F.
    Cordasco. New York: McGraw-Hill, 1973. A brief
    history with notices of the mainland experience.

Mills, C. Wright; Clarence Senior; and Rose Goldsen. The Puerto Ri-
    can Journey: New York's Newest Migrant. Harper, 1950. Re-
    issued, New York, Russell & Russell, 1969. A carefully re-
    searched field study of the Puerto Rican population in two core
    areas of New York City. The study was done in 1948 by a re-
    search team of the bureau of applied social research of Colum-
    bia University. Although many of its statistics are now out-of-

date, the book deals with basic concepts, such as the factors in "adaptation," cultural and language differences, and their influence on the progress and problems of the migrants. Includes much data on the characteristics of the Puerto Ricans in the two core areas -- family, age, sex, education, occupation, income, etc.

Pico, Rafael, Nueva Geografia de Puerto Rico: Fisica, Economica, y Social. Rio Piedras: University of Puerto Rico Press, 1969. The most complete geography of the island; an English translation is in preparation.

Puerto Rican Community Development Project. Puerto Rican Forum (New York), 1964. This report was developed as the basis for an anti-poverty, economic opportunity project, and is subtitled "A Proposal for a Self-Help Project to Develop the Community by Strengthening the Family, Opening Opportunities for Youth and Making Full Use of Education." The forum is a private agency, with a professional and secretarial staff of New Yorkers of Puerto Rican background. It has received some financial support from foundations to develop self-help projects, as well as some public money to develop its proposal. Thus the concern in this report is to highlight the problems -- income, housing, education, family, etc. -- that confront the Puerto Rican community in New York City, though not all of its population. Data are presented to support the thesis that Puerto Ricans generally are not well off and need to make much more rapid gains in a contemporary technical, urban society such as New York. As a Forum summary indicates, the report is advanced as a rationale for a project "which takes into consideration both the problems of poverty in New York City and the complex realities of the cultural community pattern of the Puerto Rican New Yorker." The report is not intended to be a rounded picture of the total Puerto Rican population in New York City. Read from the point of view of its purpose, it is an illuminating study.

"(The) Puerto Rican Experience on the United States Mainland," International Migration Review, vol. II (Spring 1968). Entire issue devoted to a comprehensive account of the experience.

Sexton, Patricia. Spanish Harlem: Anatomy of Poverty. Harper & Row, 1965. Report by a sociologist who spent part of two years "getting acquainted" with East Harlem. Shows awareness that she is dealing with the pathologies of a minority of the area's population ("still, the majority of the people are self-supporting").

However, she does not gloss over the problems that confront many of the self-supporting, low-income urban dwellers. The book is informed by the important insight of the need for "the poor" to be involved in working out their destiny. See F. Cordasco, "Nights in the Gardens of East Harlem: Patricia Sexton's East Harlem," Journal of Negro Education, vol. 34 (Fall 1965), pp. 450-451; and F. Cordasco, "Spanish Harlem: The Anatomy of Poverty, "Phylon: The Atlanta Review of Race & Culture, vol. 26 (Summer 1965), pp. 195-196.

Status of Puerto Rico. Report of the United States--Puerto Rico Commission on the Status of Puerto Rico. Washington: U. S. Government Printing Office, 1966. Includes "Selected Bibliography" (Legal-Constitutional; Political; Economic; Social-Cultural-Historical; Government Publications) with some annotation.'

Status of Puerto Rico. Selected Background Studies Prepared for the United States--Puerto Rico Commission on the Status of Puerto Rico. Washington, D. C.: U. S. Government Printing Office, 1966. (Includes Clarence Senior and Donald O. Watkins, "Toward A Balance Sheet of Puerto Rican Migration: Bibliography.")

Vivas, José Luis. Historia de Puerto Rico. New York: Las Americas Publishing Co., 1962. The best brief contemporary history available in Spanish.

Wagenheim, Kal. Puerto Rico: A Profile. New York: Praeger, 1970.

Wells, Henry. The Modernization of Puerto Rico: A Political Study of Changing Values and Institutions. Cambridge, Mass.: Harvard University Press, 1969. Analysis of the "Muñoz Era."

III EDUCATION

Anderson, Virginia. "Teaching English to Puerto Rican Pupils," High Points (March 1964), pp. 51-54.

Bilingual Education: Hearings, U.S. Senate, Committee on Labor and Public Welfare. Special Sub-Committee on Bilingual Education, 90th Congress, 1st Session. Washington: U.S. Government Printing Office, Part I, May 1967; Part II, June 1967. On Title VII (Elementary and Secondary Education Act) which was enacted in 1968.

"Bilingualism," The Center Forum, vol. 4, (September 1969). Entire issue is given to analysis of Title VII (Elementary and Secondary Education Act), programs and related matters. Includes an important annotated bibliography.

Bucchioni, Eugene. A Sociological Analysis of the Functioning of Elementary Education for Puerto Rican Children in the New York City Public Schools. Unpublished doctoral dissertation, New School for Social Research, 1965.

Cordasco, Francesco. "The Puerto Rican Child in the American School." American Sociological Association Abstract of Papers, 61st Annual Meeting (1966), pp. 23-24.

Cordasco, Francesco. "Puerto Rican Pupils and American Education." School & Society, vol. 95 (February 18, 1967), pp. 116-119. Also, with some change, in Journal of Negro Education (Spring 1967); and Kansas Journal of Sociology, vol. 2 (Spring 1966), pp. 59-65.

Cordasco, Francesco. "The Challenge of the Non-English Speaking Child in the American School" School & Society, vol. 96 (March 30, 1968), pp. 198-201. On the proposal for the enactment of the Bilingual Education Act. (Title VII, Elementary and Secondary Education Act), with historical background.

Cordasco, Francesco. "Educational Pelagianism: The Schools and the Poor," Teachers College Record, vol. 69 (April 1968), pp. 705-709.

Cordasco, Francesco and Eugene Bucchioni. The Puerto Rican Community of Newark, N. J.: An Educational Program for its Children. Newark: Board of Education, Summer 1970. A detailed report on the implementation of a program for Puerto Rican students.

Cordasco, Francesco and E. Bucchioni. Education Programs for Puerto Rican Students. (Jersey City Public Schools). Evaluation and Recommendations. Jersey City: Board of Education, 1971.

Cordasco, F. and Eugene Bucchioni. Newark Bilingual Education Program, 1970-1971. Newark: Board of Education, 1971. Evaluation report of a massive program for Puerto Rican students.

Cordasco, Francesco and Eugene Bucchioni. The Puerto Rican Com-
     munity and its Children on the Mainland: A Sourcebook for
     Teachers, Social Workers and other Professionals. Metuchen,
     N.J.: Scarecrow Press, 2nd ed., 1972. "The original struc-
     turing of the text has been retained, and it is within this frame-
     work that new materials have been interpolated. New materials
     have been added to Part I (Aspects of Puerto Rican Culture)
     whose basic design is to afford a politico-cultural kaleidoscope
     of island life; to Part II (The Puerto Rican Family), bringing
     into clear focus the family's transition to mainland life; to Part
     III (The Puerto Rican Experience on the Mainland: Conflict and
     Acculturation), in bringing into sharp view the new politiciza-
     tion of the mainland experience; and in Part IV (The Puerto Ri-
     can Experience on the Mainland: Puerto Rican Children in
     North American Schools) in affording additional materials on
     bilingual education and in providing outlines for course content
     and staff-training. Appended to the bibliography are selected
     additional references." (Preface to the 2nd ed.)

Cordasco, Francesco and Eugene Bucchioni, "A Staff Institute for Tea-
     chers of Puerto Rican Students," School & Society, vol. 99
     (Summer 1972).

Diaz, Manuel and Roland Cintrón. School Integration and Quality Edu-
     cation: New York: Puerto Rican Forum, 1964.

Hemos Trábajado Bien. A Report on the First National Conference of
     Puerto Ricans, Mexican-Americans and Educators on the
     Special Educational Needs of Puerto Rican Youth (New York:
     Aspira, 1968). Includes a series of recommendations.

John, Vera P. and Vivian M. Horner. Early Childhood Bilingual Educa-
     tion (New York: Modern Language Association 1971). Invalu-
     able. Includes a "Typology of Bilingual Education Models;"
     excellent documentation and bibliography.

Margolis, Richard J. The Losers: A Report on Puerto Ricans and the
     Public Schools (New York: Aspira, 1968). An important report
     on visits to a number of schools with description and evaluation
     of programs for Puerto Rican children.

(Puerto Rican Children) "Education of Puerto Rican Children in New
     York City," The Journal of Educational Sociology, vol. 28
     (December 1954), pp. 145-192. An important collection of arti-
     cles.

Morrison, J. Cayce, Director. The Puerto Rican Study: 1953-57. New
    York City Board of Education, 1958. Final report of the most
    complete study of the impact of Puerto Rican migration on the
    public schools of New York City, and how schools were affect-
    ing Puerto Rican children and their parents. Though sponsored
    by the New York City Board of Education, matching grant-in-
    aid of half a million dollars from the Fund for the Advancement
    of Education made the study possible. Specialized studies were
    done within the framework of the large-scale study. These
    smaller studies focused on the "socio-cultural adjustment" of
    the children and their parents, and digests are presented in
    final report. About a third of the book deals with the special
    non-English-speaking program developed by the city school
    system. Description of some of the methods and materials de-
    veloped is included. Study discovered some unresolved prob-
    lems in the areas of learning, effective grouping of pupils,
    staffing those schools with Puerto Rican children, and teacher
    education. Study led to many research and curriculum publi-
    cations, and 23 major recommendations, all designed to
    achieve three purposes: "***(developing) better understand-
    ing of the children being taught, (relating) the teaching of Eng-
    lish to the child's cultural-social adjustment, (improving) the
    integration of ethnic groups through the school's program"
    (p. 247). With respect to the children, the major conclusion
    is contained in the following statement: "The children of Puerto
    Rican background are exceedingly heterogeneous. This is true
    of their native intelligence, their prior schooling, their apti-
    tude for learning English, and their scholastic ability***"
    (p. 239). Reissued with an introductory essay by F. Cordasco
    (New York: Oriole Editions, 1972).

INDEX

INDEX

135

137

TITLES IN THE
ETHNIC CHRONOLOGY SERIES